Wild Ju

The Lynn Siddons Murder

HARRY PUGH

ROBERT HALE · LONDON

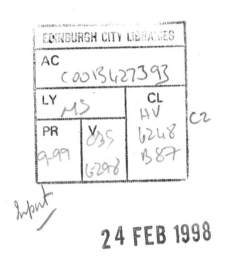
Photoset in Times by
Derek Doyle & Associates, Mold, Clwyd.
Printed in Great Britain by
St Edmundsbury Press Ltd, Bury St Edmunds, Suffolk.
Bound by WBC Bookbinders Ltd, Bridgend, Mid-Glamorgan.

Contents

Revenge is a kind of wild justice, which the more man's nature runs to, the more ought law to weed it out.

Francis Bacon
1561–1626

List of Illustrations

PICTURE CREDITS

Derby Evening Telegraph: frontispiece, 4, 9, 12, 13. BBC Photographic Library: 5, 6, 7, 10. Stephen Cornwell: 11. The *Mail on Sunday*: 14. *Daily Mirror*: 15.

Foreword

This book is not just about the life and death of Lynn Siddons who was strangled and stabbed in a frenzied attack a few months after her sixteenth birthday, the real story is her family's battle against the authorities to avenge her untimely end.

For years it looked as if her killer, Michael Brookes, would get away with murder. He was named in print and pictured on television but the police left him to walk the streets and seemed to be taking no action to arrest and charge him.

The case is bizarre. At first, his fifteen-year-old stepson, Roy Brookes, was charged with the murder. But he was acquitted after he named Michael Brookes as the killer-in-chief.

The Siddons family refused to accept that Lynn's murderer could get away without paying for his crime. They launched a bitter campaign against Michael Brookes and his family which caused them to change their names and flee into hiding.

Lynn's grandmother, Flo, is just over five feet tall; her mother, Gail, is just under five feet; and her aunt, Cynthia, is about the same size. These three little ladies, nicknamed The Three Musketeers, battled against the authorities, taking on the police and the law in a crusade that lasted almost fourteen years.

In a historic case at the Royal Courts of Justice, they won an action for damages. It was the first time the civil law had been used in this way in a murder case for which no one had been convicted. Michael Brookes was named as Lynn's killer and Roy his unwilling accomplice.

Shortly afterwards Michael Brookes was arrested and

charged. His lawyers fought for four more years to try to prevent the case from coming to court. But they lost, and after a six-and-a-half week trial at the Old Bailey, a jury found him guilty and he was sentenced to life imprisonment.

The Siddons family have triumphed in their long fight for justice. At last, Lynn's death has been avenged and she can rest in peace.

1 A Murder is Arranged

The short but happy life of Lynn Siddons came to an abrupt end at about three o'clock in the afternoon of 3 April 1978. She was walking unsuspectingly along the towpath of a canal when she was hit in the back. The arm of a strangler tightened around her neck and knives were plunged into her body a total of forty-one times.

Mercifully Lynn did not have to endure a long and painful death. Experts estimate her life ebbed away in a brief thirty seconds. But the crazed knifeman kept hacking away in a sex-driven frenzy even after she was dead, slashing her buttocks and breasts, loins and stomach.

The jolly 16-year-old was especially happy that Easter Monday. She had just left school and was looking forward to starting her first job. That evening she was planning to go to a fairground with a boyfriend. Her eyes were bright with anticipation of the fun and laughter ahead.

She had been lured on that walk to her death by a young boy who lived a few doors away from her home. It was a bitterly cold day with a scything easterly wind and a hint of sleet in the air. But Lynn agreed to accompany the boy when he said he wanted to go to a farm to ask for work. As the pair set off across the golf course towards the open countryside, she had no idea she was walking into a trap.

Lynn Siddons was murdered a couple of miles from her home at Sinfin on the outskirts of Derby. For years her killers looked like getting away with their bloody crime. Michael Brookes and his black stepson Roy were named in newspapers, magazines and on TV. But an incredible series of bungles by the police, aided and abetted by our archaic legal system, created a farcical situation which made it possible for a known murderer to remain at large for years.

Lynn's family have many times accused the pair of killing her. They mounted a ferocious vendetta against them. Her mother Gail says, 'We were determined that even if we couldn't get justice from the law, we'd make life hell for Lynn's murderers.'

And so they did. Lynn's grandmother, Flo Siddons, her mother Gail Halford, and her aunt, Cynthia Smith, three diminutive women who barely reach five feet, pursued the Brookes family with the tenacity of terriers to avenge the death of the teenage girl who meant so much to them.

Even the law had no doubt that Michael and Roy Brookes were the culprits. A High Court judge named them in court, saying that they were responsible for the attack that caused her death, and that no other person could conceivably be involved. He called it a murder, even though it was not a murder trial.

In spite of this certainty, it took more than fourteen years before the police charged Michael Brookes and another four to put him on trial. Roy was tried for Lynn's murder and acquitted shortly after the crime. But his stepfather, whose guilt seemed to be unquestioned, walked free. And he would undoubtedly still be free were it not for the persistence of Flo Siddons and her family. The unsolved case remained like an ugly stain on Derby's reputation for law and order.

The weekend Lynn died was a special one for the city. A service was held at the cathedral as part of the charter celebrations, and all sorts of dignitaries were there – mayors, councillors, city officials, magistrates – to hear the Bishop of Derby, the Rt Revd Cyril Bowles, give a moving evocation about the city and its new status.

He concluded, 'May the Grace of God enable us to grow in mutual understanding to honour and respect each other, to differ without division, and to bring new gifts of vision and integrity to the city and its people.'

While the bishop was uttering his inspiring message, there was precious little honour or respect in the mind of Michael Brookes as he sat in his squalid home plotting Lynn's murder. His hobby was pinning up photographs of naked women he tore from soft-porn magazines and stabbing them in the breasts and buttocks. Or sometimes he would throw darts at them, giving a gleeful cry if the point hit the private parts.

Lynn had just returned from a holiday in Italy where she had gone to visit her godparents. She had brought presents for the Brookes family – cigarettes for Michael and his wife Dot, a pack of cards for Roy, a doll for Tracey. They had even sat around the table in the Brookes' household playing a game of rummy with the new cards.

Yet Roy was to show his gratitude by inviting her to a quiet spot where he knew his stepfather would be hiding to ambush the unsuspecting girl.

Lynn didn't like Mick Brookes, and he knew it. She often said she felt uneasy in his company. There was no way she would have gone for a walk in the lonely countryside if she had known he was going to be about. As her best friend Pam White says, 'Mick Brookes must have taken her by surprise. If she'd have seen him, she'd have legged it – and she was a good runner.'

But she felt safe enough with Roy. He was smaller, lighter and younger than Lynn. She wouldn't have chosen him as a friend – he couldn't read or write properly, and was no real companion for a lively intelligent girl. But she felt sorry for the boy, especially when other youths teased him and called him 'nigger'.

As they set out she would have been chatting excitedly about her holiday and her new job at the Co-op. She might have been a little put out at first – her boyfriend was supposed to meet her but hadn't turned up. But Lynn would have soon got over that as the pair pulled their coats around them to shield them from the wind and strode purposefully across the fields.

Their walk took them through a copse known as Red Wood, and over a small footbridge, along the edge of a field where the barley shoots were just peeping through the soil and on to a lane. It was here they were joined by Mick Brookes. Lynn would not have been pleased, but Mick must have made it appear as if the meeting was a coincidence so as not to arouse her suspicions.

The trio then passed two farms but didn't call at either. By this time Lynn must have been getting a little impatient,

'Where is this farm then? Are you sure it's down here? Did the farmer say there would definitely be work?'

All Mick Brookes had told his stepson was that he had spoken to a man sitting on a wall who had told him there was work to be had at one of the farms. It was an obvious lie, and if Lynn had known anything about farming she would have spotted it, and maybe been put on her guard. It had been a cold winter, and the ground was still frozen. There was no work to be done at that time in the fields.

They passed yet another farm, Moores Farm, and again didn't call. Perhaps Mick Brookes put Lynn's mind at rest by saying the farm where he thought there would be work was on a different route which they would pass on the way home. One hundred yards further on they came to the humped redbrick bridge over the canal. There is another bridge about half a mile along the towpath. By using this, they could get back to their homes along the different route, passing other farms. Canal bridges are numbered. The first they crossed was number 15. They went down the track to the towpath and started to walk towards bridge 16. Lynn met her death between bridges 15 and 16 on the Trent and Mersey Canal.

Part of the towpath is open to fields. Mick Brookes would not have risked killing Lynn there where he might be spotted. There is a railway track nearby where trains carry coal to the power station at Willington. Who knows? An alert engine driver might have seen the attack and warned the police. And there were some waterway workers chugging along on a barge. He would have to wait until they were out of the way. But there is a place further along where bushes and dense undergrowth grow alongside the towpath forming a natural screen. This was the spot Mick Brookes had marked for the murder. Here he knew there would be no witnesses and no interruption.

As they walked towards the bushes, Lynn was in front, with Mick just behind her and Roy following behind him. Suddenly the conversation stopped. Mick Brookes lunged forward propelling Lynn into the bushes. Her cry was cut off as he roughly grabbed her and cupped his hand over her mouth saying, 'I've got a present for you.'

Lynn was a well-built girl but no match for Mick Brookes,

who is six foot one inch tall with large hands and feet and a simian build. She struggled, but by this time Brookes had got his arm around her neck. Gritting his teeth ferociously, he snarled at Roy, 'Take this knife. Stick it in her.'

The terrified boy took the black-handled carving knife. He didn't want to hurt Lynn but he was scared of his stepfather. He stabbed her, but gently, hardly pricking the skin through her shirt and jeans. Then he pressed the knife against her stomach so the handle broke and the blade clattered to the ground.

By now the girl's body hung limply. Mick Brookes, while maintaining his stranglehold, took another knife which Roy had been carrying. Time after time, he plunged it into Lynn's body – through her jeans into her buttocks, into her stomach, into her chest. Sometimes the blade sank in up to four inches.

Roy Brookes watched his stepfather as he kept raining down blows in a *Psycho*-style rhythm of violence. The boy had seen him like this before, only then it was with pictures from girlie magazines or underwear catalogues. He had heard Mick Brookes boasting he would like to kill more women than Jack the Ripper. When they had gone walking together, his stepfather had said after passing women he would like to grab them and stab them to death.

That was talk – but this was for real. The boy was petrified. He wanted to run away but his legs wouldn't move. He remained rooted to the spot, hypnotized by terror, as the knife blows continued thudding into Lynn's limp body. Then Brookes dragged the body to a puddle of muddy water on the towpath. He pressed her face into it with his foot. Even then he wasn't satisfied. He scooped up a handful of mud and leaf mould and thrust it into her mouth.

With Roy looking on still shaking with fear, Mick Brookes held the body under the arms and dragged it deep into the thick undergrowth where it would not be easily found. But before he left it, he hoisted up her brassiere over her breasts and unzipped her jeans.

It was a crude attempt to make it look as if Lynn had been the victim of a sex attack. But it fooled nobody. Her panties, though holed four times by the knife blade, were still in position, as was the sanitary towel she was wearing.

Michael Brookes then sloped off along the towpath, his stepson following him. He may have been gratified sexually by the rhythm of the knife sinking into Lynn's flesh – but the deed he performed that cheerless afternoon would haunt him for years to come.

2 'Where's Lynn?'

On the morning of the day she died, Lynn Siddons was in her usual good spirits, even though she was still tired after the long overnight rail journey from Milan where she had gone with her mother and grandmother to visit her godparents.

She was due to start work the next week packing cooked meats in the butchery department of the Co-operative Wholesale Society in Osmaston Road, Derby, and on the Monday morning she went into Derby with her grandmother, Flo Siddons, and her aunt, Cynthia Smith, to buy some clothes for her new job.

Lynn had left school at sixteen before taking her O levels. Schoolfriends and teachers thought she was a bright girl who hadn't worked hard enough to reach her potential. Even though she was eagerly looking forward to the Co-op job, those who knew her well felt it was just a temporary post, and that she would soon move on to a career where she could use her amenable nature and skills at getting on with people to better advantage.

She was also looking forward to a date. With her bubbling enthusiasm for excitement and laughter, she loved funfairs. The Easter fair was on in Derby that evening and she was going to enjoy the noise, flashing lights and fast rides with a boyfriend, Bobby Muir, whom she had arranged to meet in the early afternoon.

But first, the shopping trip. She went with her grandmother and aunt into Ranbys, one of Derby's main department stores. But at about 11.30 a.m. she left them saying she wanted to go to Littlewoods to buy some black pants and tights and would then catch the bus home.

When they arrived at Carlyle Street at about 2.30 p.m.,

Flo and Cynthia didn't know whether Lynn would be there or not. But when they saw her red purse on the window-sill, they knew she had not yet left for the fair. They assumed she had gone to see one of her friends who lived nearby. If ever she went out for any length of time, she invariably left a note saying where she had gone and when she would be back.

Cynthia stayed with her mother until about 4 p.m. then left to drive to her own home in Tivoli Gardens across the city. Flo started to prepare the tea. She found herself wondering where Lynn could be. It was strange that she hadn't left a note. She always left a note.

After half an hour she decided she must do something. She put on her coat and went up to the Brookes' house to ask them if they had seen anything of Lynn.

The difference between the two houses, though they are both built of red brick and are in the same street, was quite remarkable. Flo Siddons's home, number 1, was neat, clean and immaculate. The Brookes house, number 27, was dirty and dilapidated with scruffy curtains, smudged windows and unkempt hedges and gardens.

Flo knocked at the door. It was answered by Mick Brookes' wife, Doris, whom everyone called Dot. 'Have you seen our Lynn?' asked Flo.

'No,' Dot said. 'Isn't she back?'

Flo shook her head. 'I can't understand it. She always leaves a note if she's going to be gone any length of time.'

Dot said she thought Lynn had gone off with Roy to look for a part-time job on one of the farms. She said, 'I heard Mick talking about it. He's had a word with someone who is looking for youngsters for part-time work.'

'Is Roy back?' asked Flo.

'Yes, he's been back. But I don't know where he is now,' said Dot

Flo walked back down the road to her own home. She tried to eat her tea, but the growing worry had removed her appetite. Then she went out again – to the house where Lynn's friend Pat Broadhead lived around the corner in Thackeray Street.

It was there she learned that Bobby Muir, Lynn's boyfriend, had not turned up for their date. Bobby was in a bit of trouble with the police over some petty thefts. The police wanted to interview him, and he was trying to keep out of their way.

Pat had also been out that afternoon, or Lynn would have almost certainly called at her house, and probably stayed listening to records. The two girls had met when they had started school together at Sinfin Primary School and had remained close friends. Their bedrooms faced each other across the street, and on summer nights they would leave the windows open and shout goodnight to each other before going to sleep.

When Bobby hadn't turned up for their date, Lynn had gone to call for Pat. When there was no reply, she had gone to the Brookes' house. And that was when Roy Brookes had asked her to go with him to look for work on the farm, waiting for her to nip home to change into her boots for the walk across the fields.

Flo waited until later in the evening, her anxiety growing by the minute. Another unanswered question: If Lynn had gone for a walk, why hadn't she taken Lassie? Whenever she went across the fields, she took her black and white collie with her? But Lassie was in the house.

She felt she must do something – so she decided on another visit to the Brookes' house. Perhaps Roy would be back by now. He might know something of Lynn's movements.

Back she went along the street to scruffy number 27. Again she knocked at the door. This time Roy was there. Flo began to quiz him about when he had last seen Lynn, and where they had gone together.

Mick Brookes, Roy and Lynn had left the house together, he said. Mick Brookes had walked the opposite way to them along Carlyle Street. They had made their way to Thackeray Street and the golf course. Mick had gone in the other direction, the boy said, giving them a wave from the end of the street.

'Where did you go then?' Flo persisted.

'We went past Red Wood, and I went into the wood for a pee. When I came out, Lynn had vanished.'

Flo was dubious. 'She just went off without saying anything?'

Roy nodded his head. 'Yes.'

Flo said, 'Didn't you see her when you came out? There are fields all round. You'd be able to see anyone walking away from the woods. Which way did she go?'

Roy insisted that he hadn't seen her going – that she had just vanished. Flo was not happy with this explanation for Lynn's disappearance, but there was nothing else she could say. The boy's story just didn't add up. The seeds of a growing suspicion began to take root in her mind. As she turned the words over and over, she began to shiver with a nameless fear that Lynn had come to some harm.

Slowly, she walked along the street to the telephone kiosk. The Siddons family had always been close, and whenever there was trouble they all rallied round.

The first number Flo rang was her eldest son Keith at Littleover. He hadn't seen or heard anything of Lynn, but he said he'd drive over right away and pick up Gail, Lynn's mother, on the way.

Then Flo rang Gail. She hadn't seen Lynn since their Sunday lunch together the previous day. She said she would come round with Keith and stay with her mother. Gail had given birth to Lynn when she was just seventeen and unmarried. But it was Flo who had brought up the baby. Lynn always called Flo 'Mam', and she thought of Gail more as a sister.

Flo then tried to ring Cynthia. But Cynthia was at a friend's birthday party and couldn't be contacted until much later. But she hadn't seen anything of Lynn since the shopping trip earlier in the day. Flo also rang her younger son Barrie, but he hadn't seen or heard anything of Lynn either.

As the minutes ticked by while she waited for her son and daughter to arrive, Flo sat in the lounge gazing at the settee where Lynn normally sat, her legs curled under her as she watched TV or listened to her records. Flo was completely mystified. Lynn was a considerate girl who would never cause her family unnecessary worry. This lengthening absence was completely out of character. When they arrived, Keith and Gail agreed something must have happened to prevent her getting home – or getting in touch with them. So, at 10 p.m., they decided to call the police.

Gail told them Lynn was missing, and a uniformed

constable arrived at the house shortly afterwards. He listened to the story, but did not seem unduly perturbed. After all, thousands of teenage girls go missing every week. Most of them run off with their boyfriends, or head off to the bright lights of London. They nearly always turn up after a few days.

Even when Flo said Lynn had gone without taking her purse or spare clothes, he still didn't seem bothered. 'It's too dark to do anything tonight,' he said. 'We'll have a look around in the morning.'

The Siddons family knew Lynn hadn't run away with her boyfriend, or by herself. 'She just wasn't the sort of girl to do that,' Flo says. 'But the more we told that to the police, the less they seemed to believe us. Yet anybody who knew Lynn, not just the family but her friends as well, would know she wouldn't simply run away – and that something serious must have happened to her.'

Gail stayed with her mother that night, and slept in the same bed to comfort her. Since her husband Fred had died suddenly the previous Christmas, Lynn always slept with her grandmother. But this night Gail took her place.

In spite of the warm companionship of her daughter, Flo couldn't sleep. She tossed and turned and whenever she began to doze off, a fresh wave of worries would crowd into her mind. Then she realized Gail wasn't asleep either. The pair of them could hear the wind blowing outside, and they knew it was bitterly cold. Flo whispered to her daughter, 'If Lynn's out in this, she'll never survive. She'll die of exposure.'

'I know, 'Gail said. 'It's freezing out there.'

'Supposing she's injured, and can't move,' Flo said. 'What if she's lying out there helpless.'

'What can we do?' asked Gail.

It was 2 a.m. but they decided they had to do something. The pair of them put on dressing gowns and went downstairs. Flo made a cup of tea and then went out with Gail to the telephone kiosk. First she rang Keith. He had just got into bed, but sensing his mother's distress he instantly agreed to come back round to see what he could do. And Barrie, who also lived in Littleover, arrived at Carlyle Street about the same time.

Keith and Barrie wrapped themselves in scarves and thick coats, took flashlights and went out into the wild wintry night to search for Lynn. They also took Lassie.

The two men walked down Thackeray Street and along Wilmore Road. There was nobody about to ask except the gatekeeper at the Rolls Royce factory in Wilmore Road. He hadn't seen anything, so the two men headed off to Red Wood where, according to the story Roy Brookes had told, Lynn had last been seen. Keith remembers:

> I knew the woods well. I used to play there as a boy. It's only a small wood, but it's criss-crossed with scores of tracks and the undergrowth is quite dense in places. It was a terrible night with the wind howling through the trees. We searched and searched, but couldn't find anything. We knew Lassie would find her if she was lying in the woods.

They returned to Carlyle Street a couple of hours later, and told Flo and Gail they had found nothing. It was not surprising. Lynn's body was lying in its cold and lonely resting place at least two miles from where they had been searching.

3   Something to Hide

The days which followed were an agony for Flo Siddons. At night she couldn't sleep, and the daylight hours were filled with doubts and anxiety.

One of her main frustrations was the attitude of the police. Whenever she said she thought some harm had come to Lynn, the police officers kept insisting, 'Don't worry. She's run off with that Bobby Muir. When we find him, we'll find her.' The more she tried to reason with them that Lynn just wasn't the sort of girl to run off, especially as she had not taken any spare clothes or money, the less convinced they seemed to be.

Policemen play these things by the book, and the book says that when teenage girls or boys go missing, they've run away – and they always come back after a few days. The book also says that parents and grandparents nearly always maintain their child is not the sort to run away. But they're wrong. The book says they are wrong.

The police did carry out a token search for Lynn – just one officer and a dog. He walked around Red Wood and searched the neighbouring fields. Just like Keith and Barrie he found nothing.

The police officers also spoke to Roy Brookes as the last person known to have seen Lynn. But he stuck to his story that she had gone off while he was having a pee in the wood, and they seemed satisfied with that.

On the Tuesday afternoon – the day after Lynn vanished – Roy and his mother Dot called at the Siddons house. Roy had a new story to tell. With much prompting by his mother, the boy said that when he had come out of the wood, he couldn't see Lynn anywhere – but he had seen a white car.

Flo knew the woods well. She had taken her children for

walks there when they were younger. When they were late for their tea, she had often gone there to call them and bring them home. She knew they were surrounded by fields, and no vehicle, unless it was a farm tractor, could get to them.

'A car?' she said. 'How could a car get across the fields? You're a little liar. There was no car. There couldn't have been a car.' Roy kept mumbling that he had seen a car, but Flo Siddons was getting cross so his mother quickly ushered him from her house and back up the street to their own house.

Alone, Flo began to ponder. What a strange thing for the lad to say. Why should he lie? She knew Roy had learning difficulties and couldn't read properly, or write. But why should he invent things? Was it some silly little game he was playing? Or could there be a more sinister reason?

Her thoughts were interrupted by the arrival of Cynthia. She told her daughter about Roy's curious remark and the pair of them decided to go up to the Brookes' house to give the boy a thorough quizzing.

When they arrived Roy told them Mick and his mother were in the bath together. But Dot appeared in her dressing gown as soon as Flo and Cynthia began asking Roy questions, and Mick Brookes soon followed her into the cluttered living room where there were dirty pots and pans on the table and an Alsatian bitch with a litter of puppies in the corner.

Cynthia asked, 'What were you and Lynn talking about when you were walking to the woods?'

'Films we'd seen on the telly,' Roy replied.

'What else?'

The boy began to mumble, and Mick Brookes kept butting in. It seemed as if he wanted to keep control of the conversation without letting Roy say too much. But the two women kept shooting questions at him even though most of the time they were not getting replies.

'Did Lynn say she was going anywhere?' Flo asked.

Mick Brookes interjected. 'I think she's run away with that chap Bobby.'

'Why should she without telling us?' said Flo.

Then Brookes dropped a bombshell. 'Well, she didn't tell you everything. She used to sneak out at night to meet

Bobby. They used to kip in an empty house in Harrington Street.'

'That's a lie,' said Flo. 'She's been sleeping with me ever since my husband died at Christmas.'

'She used to wait until you were asleep and climb over you,' said Brookes.

'She couldn't have done anything of the sort,' Flo retorted. 'I'm a light sleeper. I'd wake up if she moved.'

Her temper rising, Cynthia said, 'Why are you slagging her off like this? She's a thoroughly decent girl, and you know it.'

Brookes sneered, 'That's what you think – but I know differently.'

The conversation was making Flo and Cynthia extremely angry. This man was suggesting Lynn was a slut who slept around. They both knew this to be completely false. Why was he saying it? Flo also knew there were no empty houses in Harrington Street. So why was Brookes lying?

When they returned home, Flo and Cynthia discussed what Brookes had said, and Flo said to her daughter, 'Roy Brookes told a lie about the car. Mick Brookes told lies about Lynn. Why are they lying? What have they got to hide?'

'Do you think they might have done something to Lynn?' asked Cynthia.

Flo thought hard. 'I don't know. But I don't trust either of them. What reason can they have for lying?'

That evening, and on the evenings to follow, there was no time for theorizing. Lynn's disappearance demanded action. They didn't seem to be getting very much from the police who were still convinced the missing girl was just another teenage runaway. So the Siddons family decided to do a little bit of police work themselves.

Armed with Lynn's photograph, Flo went with her two daughters and two sons to the fair where Lynn was planning to go with Bobby Muir the night she vanished. The family split up, showing the picture of the smiling girl to stallholders, the men who took the money at the rides and roundabouts, the candy floss sellers, the bingo callers.

They moved among the laughing, jostling crowds flashing Lynn's picture at anyone who might have seen her. But nobody had seen her. Lynn had not been anywhere near the fair. She was lying dead in the damp undergrowth.

The Siddons visited the fairground at night. And they were just as busy in the daytime. They put on rubber boots to trudge around Sinfin Moor, crossing the muddy fields and lanes where Lynn had gone on her last walk. They showed her picture to farmers, horseriders, joggers, ramblers, but nobody had seen her.

One evening, after they had returned home tired to Carlyle Street, Roy Brookes knocked at the door.

'Has anything been seen of Lynn?'he asked.

Flo Siddons shook her head.

'Can you lend me a picture of her?'Roy asked. 'I'd like to go around and see if I can help to find her.'

Flo felt herself melting a little towards the pathetic little boy. Perhaps he wasn't such a bad lad after all, even if he had told that silly lie. She gave him a copy of Lynn's passport picture and off he went saying he would try to find her.

Curiously, there was no mention of Lynn's disappearance in the media, even though Flo had pleaded with the police that it might help to trace her. She had even offered to pay for an advertisement, but the police were adamant that it would do no good.

During the six days she was missing, the *Derby Evening Telegraph* reported how high-speed trains made in the city had hit a world record of 143 mph, how the MP for Derby South, Walter Johnson, was complaining about the disgraceful profiteering by chip shops (15p for a portion that should cost 8p) and even how the Women's Institute at Chaddeston had been given a talk on making corn dollies. But there was no mention of Lynn Siddons, not even a paragraph. The newspaper was unaware of the drama that was being played out at Sinfin on the southern edge of the city.

Even though Roy Brookes called every evening to see if there was any news and made out he was deeply concerned, Flo and other members of the Siddons family still harboured a niggling suspicion that he was not as innocent as he seemed. More than once Flo asked detectives who called if they had considered Roy might have done some harm to Lynn. But the police officers dismissed the suggestion: 'You can see the size of him? How could a puny little blighter like that have done anything to her?'

It was true. Roy, fifteen years old, was barely five foot tall. Lynn was several inches taller, a couple of stone heavier, and much more powerful. When they had played together, some of Lynn's friends remember her twirling him round and round like a feather pillow. There was no way that he unaided could have harmed her.

Late on the Thursday night, after they had gone to bed, the Siddons had another caller. They heard a whistle outside the house – then a second whistle. Flo Siddons was already awake. She went to the bedroom window and saw two young men in the shadows below.

'Who is it?' she called.

'It's Bobby – Bobby Muir. I've come to see about Lynn.'

Flo and Gail quickly dressed and went downstairs. They opened the door. Bobby was there with a friend. The 16-year-old lad had heard Lynn was missing, and he wondered if there was anything he could do to help.

He had come late at night, he said, because the police were looking for him. This was the young man whom police were so certain Lynn had run away with. The words of the detectives came flashing into Flo's mind, 'If we find Bobby, we'll find Lynn.'

Flo invited Bobby and his friend into the house. She felt sure he had nothing to do with Lynn's disappearance. He had called because he obviously cared about her. But, in view of what the police had said, Flo decided to report him.

While she kept Bobby talking, Gail slipped out and telephoned the police. Flo still regrets that action. She says, 'I felt awful handing him over to the police like that. But he forgave me and we became friends. He knew I only did it because I was desperate.'

A police car arrived and they took the protesting young man to Pear Tree station where they quizzed him for most of the night. But he was innocent and eventually managed to convince the detectives he hadn't seen Lynn on the day she vanished and had nothing to do with her disappearance.

With each passing day, the family felt the increasing strain. Gail had moved in with her mother, and Cynthia called in every evening after first inquiring at the police

station to see if there was any news. As they talked and
talked about what might have happened, again their
suspicions focused on the family up the street.

'Why did the boy tell those lies?' asked Flo.

Gail was just as angry as her mother and sister about the
way Mick Brookes had denigrated Lynn. Again, lies had
been told. Why?

Detectives called regularly at the Siddons' house, and Flo
told one of them, Chief Inspector Jim Payne, of her
suspicions about the Brookes.

She said, 'He's told lies about Lynn.'

The detective asked, 'Why is he lying? Why should he
lie?'

Flo simply replied, 'You tell me!'

The angriest member of the family was Cynthia. Her fury
mounted so that she was unable to contain it. One afternoon
she stormed out of the house and marched purposefully up
the street, banging loudly at the Brookes' door. It was
answered by Dot Brookes.

Her eyes blazing, Cynthia said, 'We're fed up with you lot
and the things you've said about Lynn. You're not really
interested in finding her. Give me that picture back we gave
to Roy. I want it now.'

Dot stood there looking at her. But she made no move to
get the photograph.

'Go on,' Cynthia screamed. 'Get it. My dad always carried
that picture, and he's dead. We want it back. Fetch it now.'

Again Dot hesitated.

'And we want those cards Lynn brought from Italy as
well. You're not interested in her. Give them back to us.'

Dot looked at her coldly. 'You can go to hell,' she said,
and slammed the door.

The Siddons family felt the police should have been more
active, although, with no clues to Lynn's whereabouts, it's
difficult to see exactly what they could have done. The
police, unfortunately, did not share their conviction that the
Brookes family might somehow be involved, otherwise they
might have put more pressure on them.

To the case-hardened coppers, it was just another missing
teenager like the hundreds that occur every week. And they
were still playing it by the book. She'd turn up when she got

tired of living rough and began to yearn for the comforts of her nice warm home.

But Cynthia had an idea. The MP for her constituency Derby North was a lively man called Phillip Whitehead. He held regular Friday night surgeries. Cynthia went to see him. Phillip Whitehead, a writer and TV producer, with contacts in the media, was appalled no publicity had been given to the girl's disappearance. He immediately set about rectifying the matter.

The next day, Saturday 8 April, descriptions of Lynn were broadcast on local radio. An appeal went out over the loudspeakers at The Baseball, Derby County's football ground. Derby, known as The Rams, were playing Wolverhampton Wanderers whom they beat 3-1. At last the *Derby Evening Telegraph* caught up with the story and made it their front-page lead.

Under the headlines 'Concern over Derby Girl, 16. Lynn missing since Monday', the paper printed the following report:

Concern is growing for a missing girl who disappeared from her Derby home on Monday without money or a change of clothing.

Sixteen-year-old Lynn Siddons of Carlyle Street was last seen when she went out at 2 p.m. on Monday. Derby police have now exhausted all inquiries among friends and relatives and are making a public appeal for help.

Lynn, who has just finished school, was at first thought to have been with a man when she disappeared, but police have traced him and ruled him out of the inquiry.

Det. Inspector Jim Payne, head of Pear Tree CID said today: 'We are now becoming increasingly concerned for Lynn's safety, especially in view of the fact that when she left she took no money or clothing apart from what she was wearing.

'Anybody who has seen her or who knows where she might be could help us and her parents by coming forward,' he added.

Lynn, who has never left home before, is about 5' 5" tall, of slim build, with auburn, shoulder-length hair and a pale complexion.

She was wearing blue jeans, a blue and white shirt, a red T shirt, and a blue and white sports coat.

Any information about Lynn can be passed to the police on Derby 40224.

The police had known all week that Lynn had no money or spare clothes when she disappeared, but they didn't seem concerned. It's strange how their concern increased with a little bit of political and media pressure.

4   An Open-and-shut Case!

A cadet in the Metropolitan Police Force on leave at his parents' home in Derby chanced upon the body of Lynn Siddons at 4.30 p.m. on Sunday 9 April.

Ian Hardwick, 17, was out cycling with his brother and a friend. They parked their bikes by bridge number 16 on the Trent and Mersey Canal and went walking along the towpath.

Ian found an axe handle and flung it spinning into the bushes. When he went to retrieve it in the dense wet undergrowth, he saw a bundle of clothes. At first, he thought it was a discarded Guy Fawkes. When he went closer, he saw a face with wide staring eyes and a dribble of mud coming from the mouth.

He said later, 'For some reason I thought it was a dummy. It could be because the skin was stretched tight and looked like plastic.'

He touched her right foot with his own right foot, and only then realized it was the body of a young woman. His training had taught him exactly what to do – touch nothing, phone the police.

'Quickly,' he said to his companions. 'It's a body. We must get to a phone.'

The three of them ran to the bridge and along the road to the first house. It wasn't on the phone, but nearby was a taxi driver. Ian told him of their grim discovery, and as he drove off to phone the police the three young men returned to the canal side to stand guard.

Lynn had lain on the cold, wet ground between the canal and the railway line for six lonely days before she was discovered. Soon the canal bank was buzzing with police officers. The everyday case of a missing girl had suddenly become a murder investigation.

At first detectives thought the savage wounds had been inflicted by a shotgun. But a closer examination showed she had been stabbed to death, and stabbed ferociously.

At that stage they had no idea she had also been strangled. Had they known this, the entire course of the Lynn Siddons case would have turned out differently. It would have been obvious that a small boy, acting alone, could not possibly have been responsible for simultaneously strangling and stabbing her.

But it was not until much later when her body had been moved to the mortuary at Derby Royal Infirmary and examined by the eminent Home Office pathologist, Professor Alan Usher, that this information emerged. By then, Roy Brookes had been charged with her murder. The die had been cast.

While Dr Usher was carrying out the post mortem and puzzling over the curious pattern of stab wounds – some were deep savage cuts penetrating to a depth of four inches, others mere pinpricks – the Siddons family were sitting in Flo's home in Carlyle Street.

The knock at the door came shortly before 11 p.m. Two CID officers were standing on the step. They broke the news as gently as they could.

'I'm terribly sorry,' one of them said. 'We've found a girl's body. We believe it's Lynn.'

It did not come as a surprise to Flo or the family. They had slowly prepared themselves to expect the worst. Flo says, 'I knew some harm had come to her. I'd even had a dream about her lying under bushes. She would never have gone away without telling us. After hearing nothing from her for six days, I knew in my heart that she must be dead.'

The CID officers wanted a member of the family to go with them to identify the body at the hospital. The job fell to Barrie. He did it quietly without any fuss, and he has never spoken about it, then or since. It was not a pleasant experience for him. While she had lain in the open, Lynn's pretty face had been ravaged by insects and wild animals.

There was great unhappiness at 1 Carlyle Street that night – and along the road, number 27, the Brookes household, was tearful, too. Dot Brookes broke down in a hysterical flood of tears when the police called to say Lynn's body had been found. They took Roy Brookes and his stepfather to Pear Tree police station. Two detectives, Inspector Arthur Padmore and Sergeant Peter Davidson, took Roy Brookes to an interview room. But they couldn't get anything out of him. He was sobbing uncontrollably. The tiny figure, weighing just six stone six pounds and hardly five feet tall, looked pathetic beside the large police officers.

Between bursts of tears, Roy – or Fitzroy Patrick Joseph Brookes as his full name was entered in the police records – insisted that he had gone into the wood to urinate and, when he emerged, Lynn had vanished. For more than an hour the two detectives, experts at coaxing the truth from unwilling lips, asked their probing questions. But then Roy shut up. They couldn't get another word out of him as he shuddered in convulsing sobbing fits.

The police thought it might help if his stepfather spoke to him, and Mick Brookes was allowed in to try to calm Roy. The two detectives retired for ten minutes. When they returned to the interview room, the boy who had been like a clam before was now, curiously, ready to talk.

First he said, 'You tell 'em, Dad.' But then he started talking. The words came out hesitantly and with long pauses. But it was all there – the confession the police had been hoping for.

Roy said that while they were out on the walk, Lynn had put her hand between his legs and taunted him with being sexually impotent. She had lifted up her shirt and bra, and asked him to touch her breasts. She had jeered at him and called him 'nigger'. He had become enraged. He seized the carving knife he carried, and started plunging it into her. When she was dead, he had dragged her body into the undergrowth and hoped she would not be found. No one had been there, and no one witnessed the murder.

The statement ran to just one page. As Roy Brookes could not read or write, his halting words were written down by one of the officers. Then Roy signed it in his squiggly handwriting.

It was 1.55 a.m. The police officers had had a long hard evening. Altogether, they had been quizzing Roy Brookes for three hours and twenty-five minutes.

Now they had a confession. Part of the murder weapon had been found near the body – the black handle of the carving knife. Later that day at a special juvenile court in Derby, Roy Brookes was charged with murder. The police were jubilant. It was obviously an open-and-shut case.

If the police had nagging doubts about their case against Roy Brookes, they were not on record. When Dr Usher produced his report showing that Lynn had been strangled at the same time as she was being stabbed, the investigating officers must have wondered how such a puny youth could have done it without assistance.

Lynn was bigger, heavier and stronger. Did it not occur to the police that she could have easily overpowered Roy Brookes? Did they not wonder how a six stone weakling could drag the girl's body into the undergrowth? If they did ask themselves these obvious questions, they did not, it seems, take any positive action to find the answers. Michael Brookes was allowed to go free while Roy was remanded to the juvenile wing of Leicester Prison. He alone was charged with Lynn's murder.

The trial, at Nottingham Crown Court, was not due to start until November. Roy Brookes had more than six months to wait in his lonely cell. He became withdrawn and uncommunicative. He wouldn't speak to warders or fellow prisoners. He was so upset that on one of her visits to the jail, he wouldn't speak to his mother, which was strange because he was always very attached to her.

His solicitor, Stephen Chittenden, had to visit him regularly to try to prepare his defence. But even Mr Chittenden found it impossible to penetrate the shell Roy had retreated into. There were important questions which needed answers. But Chittenden was getting nothing from Roy. 'He just sat there answering "Sir" to everything I said to him' the lawyer said.

As the months dragged by, Roy Brookes became even more brooding and isolated. His demeanour became a matter of concern for Mr Chittenden who had begun to realize that this was not a case for lawyers but for doctors. An expert on psychiatry, consultant Tom Dorman, who worked at The Pastures Hospital at Mickleover in Derbyshire, was brought in to examine the silent, sullen youth.

Dr Dorman had dealt with similar cases in the past. He knew that when a patient developed this protective carapace around him, it was a long slow job to chip your way through. He had to win Roy's confidence before he could make any progress. It took three long sessions of warm and sensitive conversation before the boy was ready to talk.

But talk he did in the end. And the words that came slowly and reluctantly in short bursts added up to a very different story from the one he had told the police on the night he was arrested.

Mr Chittenden asked the questions and Dr Dorman made notes of Roy's answers at that vital interview just before 1 p.m. at Leicester Prison on Saturday, 7 October – one month before the trial was due to begin:

Q: Did you leave the house alone with Lynn?
A: Yes. I went alone.
Q: Did you meet up with the other person at the clump of trees?
A: No. Further on.
Q: Did you go to the toilet first?
A: Yes.
Q: Did Lynn?
A: No.
Q: Did you meet up with Lynn again?
A: Yes, we met up on the bank – there is a farm a bit further on.
Q: Before you got to the canal, did you meet any other person?
A: Yes.
Q: Did he come from in front or behind?
A: In front – he was standing there.

The statement went on to describe how the three people had been walking along the towpath in single file. At this stage, Roy Brookes was not naming the third person. It went on:

Q: Were you doing much talking?
A: I wasn't talking much.
Q: What were they saying?
A: I don't know. I was too scared.
Q: Why?

A: I knew what was going to happen.
Q: Was there chat about Lynn going to be hurt?
A: I think so.
Q: Did you plan to meet this other person before you left the house?
A: Yes.
Q: When you met up you knew what was going to happen to Lynn?
A: Yes.
Q: Were you frightened?
A: Scared stiff.
Q: Were you hanging back hoping it wouldn't happen?
A: Yes.
Q: Was Lynn a good friend?
A: Yes.
Q: Did you hope it wouldn't happen?
A: Yes.

Eventually, in this staccato fashion, the entire story emerged, and Roy Brookes was persuaded to name the third person who had joined him and Lynn on that fateful walk. It was, of course, his stepfather Michael Brookes.

Roy Brookes told how Mick often talked about Jack the Ripper, and about stabbing women. Sometimes when they went walking together, he would mutter to the boy how he would like to 'kill' or 'get' young women they passed. Roy knew about his stepfather's habit of sticking pictures of near-naked women on the walls of his room and stabbing them with a knife.

Roy said his stepfather had even threatened to 'get' his mother, Dot Brookes. That had frightened him. That was why he had agreed to lure Lynn down to the canal bank on the pretext of looking for a farm job.

When they neared the bushes, Mick Brookes said to Lynn, 'I've got something for you.' It was then that she saw the knife in his hand.

Roy Brookes said: 'They went into the bushes and then he grabbed Lynn. He was behind her. He held her over the mouth. He told me to stick the knife in, a carving knife he had given me.'

I did nothing at first. I was scared. I did not want to hurt Lynn at any time. Father told me again to stick it in. He was getting angry. I didn't want to hurt her. I didn't run away as I was frightened. He might have hurt my mam. He had said so before.

The carving knife broke. I did it sideways so it would break. Father told me to get the other knife out. I got it out. He told me to stick it in. He was still holding Lynn from behind. I did it lightly. I didn't want to hurt her and Lynn fell on the floor. Once she had fallen to the floor, I didn't touch her again.

It was a damning statement, and Mr Chittenden released it to the police and the prosecuting lawyers. The police immediately went to see Mick Brookes about his stepson's story. But Brookes dismissed it as nonsense.

The police, too, were sceptical. It wouldn't be the first time an accused person had confessed to a crime then changed his story implicating someone else.

There was also a legal difficulty. If the boy's statement was true, it would make him an accomplice – and the statement of an accomplice would not be admissible in court.

So Michael Brookes remained free, and Roy Brookes was the only person to be charged with Lynn's murder when the trial began at Nottingham. Ironically, the man who had been named as the killer-in-chief was the main witness for the prosecution.

5 Happy Days

Time dragged slowly for the Siddons family in those sad weeks leading up to the trial. They were trying to get used to life without Lynn, a sparkling, lively girl, full of fun and laughter, who had for years been the focus of so much of their activity.

Holidays were planned with Lynn in mind. Shopping trips were usually to buy something for Lynn. Lynn was always the centre of attention at family gatherings and parties. She was a bridesmaid when her mother, Gail, got married, and she played the same role at her Aunt Cynthia's wedding. But now Lynn was no more.

In spite of its tragic end Lynn Siddons' life had been a full and happy one. Yet when she was born it was touch and go whether the family would keep her. For she was illegitimate, and plans were discussed to have her adopted.

Her mother, Gail Halford, says, 'Nobody thought she would be staying. We hadn't even got a proper cot for her. She slept in a drawer.'

Gail was sixteen and working at the Co-op shoe factory in Sinfin when she discovered she was pregnant. Her parents, Flo and Fred Siddons, had an old-fashioned sense of morality, and Gail was scared to tell them. The only person she confided in was a workmate, a girl who stitched up shoes on the next bench, who also happened to be pregnant and unmarried.

The year was 1961, the start of the Swinging Sixties. Sexual freedom may have been fashionable in London, but it certainly wasn't in Sinfin. Nowadays nobody would give a second thought to an unmarried woman becoming pregnant, but even though thirty years ago the morality code wasn't as strict as in Victorian times when stern fathers would banish daughters who got into trouble, there was still a degree of shame attached to it.

Gail managed to keep her secret for six months, but then her mother guessed something was wrong. She went with Gail to the doctor, and the pregnancy was confirmed.

Flo managed to extract the name of the father from Gail's unwilling lips. He was a married man, living locally, who had taken advantage of her innocence. Flo went round to his house and gave him a piece of her mind on his irresponsibility for getting a young girl into trouble and leaving her in the lurch. Then it was time to tell Fred.

Fred Siddons had been abroad serving in Italy with the Duke of Wellington's Yorkshire Regiment when Gail herself was born. He didn't see her until she was about eighteen months old, even though he had sent letters suggesting her name. She was the apple of his eye. And now, she felt, she had let her dad down. She couldn't face telling him. She left it to her mum.

Flo chose her moment. She told him one evening after he had come home from the building site where he worked as a bricklayer and had settled down after his supper.

'I've got something to tell you, Fred ... about our Gail.' After a pause and a sharp intake of breath, she blurted it out. 'She's going to have a baby.'

Fred Siddons stiffened with shock. For several minutes he sat motionless without saying a word. Then he pushed his chair from the table and went upstairs. He stayed in the bedroom all evening, and Flo could hear him quietly sobbing.

The following morning, he came down for his breakfast as though nothing had happened. He spoke to his wife. He spoke to his elder son, Keith. He spoke to Cynthia, Gail's younger sister. But there were no words for Gail.

She recalls, 'Dad didn't speak to me for three months – not a word. If he wanted to say anything to me, he'd get mum to say it. I thought he was never going to speak to me again.'

Just before she went into Derby City Hospital to have the baby, her father gave her a wrist-watch as an early Christmas present. But he still wasn't speaking to Gail, and he got Flo to hand her the watch so that his non-speaking rule would not be compromised.

Lynn was born on 22 November, 1961, a bonny baby

weighing eight pounds, five ounces. Gail, the smallest member of the Siddons family, who is only four feet, ten-and-a-half inches tall, had problems giving birth to such a large baby and had to have surgical assistance, which meant that she needed to stay in hospital a fortnight longer than most mothers.

When her parents came to see her, she wondered what her father's reaction would be. As she guessed, he melted when he saw the little dark-haired baby in the cot by her bed.

'It's a lovely baby, lass. How are you feeling?' Fred had broken his long silence. Gail knew she had been forgiven.

Every night Fred and Flo came to see their grand-daughter, and Fred took it upon himself to attend to her registration. Without consulting Gail or Flo, he decided the baby girl should be called Lynn. Next time he visited his daughter he told her what he had done, and announced quite unequivocally his decision on the name.

'I decided to call her Lynn,' he said. 'It's a nice name. Do you like it?'

Whether she did or didn't would have made no difference. The deed had been done. 'Luckily, I did like it,' says Gail. 'I certainly didn't want another argument with Dad, but I did like it and that's what we called her.'

By the time of her christening six months later, Maria had been added as a tribute to her godparents, Frieda and her Italian husband Pino. The baby was called Maria Lynn Siddons. But the name her grandfather gave her was the one that stuck. By this time, of course, all thoughts of adoption had vanished and Lynn had become the centre of attention in a loving family that would never dream of letting her go.

She grew up calling her grandmother Mam, her grandfather Dad, and her mother Gay. Gail was more like a sister to her than a mother. She was told Gail was her real mother when she was quite young, and was offered the chance of moving in with Gail and her husband, John, after their marriage. But she chose to stay with her granny, although she spent lots of weekends and holidays with Gail and her family.

Holidays were an important event to the Siddons family. Every year Flo and Fred would go somewhere. It became easier later when Fred got a job with British Rail. There were free passes for him and cheap travel for the family, so they would go away three or four times a year.

Cornwall was their favourite spot. Lynn always enjoyed the seaside. Flo recalls a holiday in Torquay when Lynn was four. There was a Salvation Army choir singing on the beach and Lynn wanted to join in as they sang 'The Old Rugged Cross.' Her grandfather hoisted her on to his shoulders so she could see what was happening.

There were lots of holidays for Lynn. As well as going for jaunts with Fred and Flo, her Uncle Keith took her to the Isle of Wight and her Aunt Cynthia took her to Skegness. The family went several times to Tenby in South Wales, and Lynn loved the boat trips to Caldy Island where she always bought a bottle of the perfume the monks produced.

To help to pay for these holidays Flo worked part-time at the Co-op shoe factory. Bringing up Lynn involved the whole family. She went to a nursery school in the day. Cynthia or Gail would meet her and take her home.

Her best friend when she started at Sinfin Primary School was a girl who lived around the corner in Kingsley Street, Pam Stocks. By a strange quirk, it was Pam who, years later, was to introduce Lynn inadvertently to the Brookes family.

Now married and living in Chellaston, Pam White recalled those early schooldays. 'What sticks in my mind is how robust she was, good at sport, swimming, a fast runner. I remember once having a wrestle with her. She got me down and was sitting on me in seconds.'

As Lynn grew older, her personality developed. She and Pam went to different secondary schools. Lynn went to the St Thomas More Catholic School. But they remained close friends and regularly met after school.

Pam says: 'She was a very caring girl, always putting other people before herself. She was always doing nice things for her friends – buying them presents and doing them favours.'

It wasn't just towards her contemporaries that Lynn showed her caring nature. She used to help her granny sell bingo cards for charity around the area, and she got to know quite a few elderly people. She was always doing favours for them, shopping when they didn't want to go out, or just sharing a little bit of her company by sitting with them in the evenings.

Flo says: 'All the local people knew about her kindness. Sometimes she'd ask me for a packet of butter or sugar to give to some old person she knew was short. She even used to give her pocket money away to people who were hard up.'

Often, as she went with her friends up the Jitty (local dialect for an alley) to get to the recreation ground, she would shout, 'Just a minute' and dash into some old person's home to see if they needed anything, and if they did she would put that first.

But she had her mischievous side as well. She and Pam used to go to ballroom dancing classes together at The Rendezvous in Derby. Sometimes after the classes they went to the cinema. The pair of them went to see *The Sound of Music* half-a-dozen times.

Pam says, 'We knew all the songs and we began to sing them. People were shushing us, but we didn't take any notice. Next thing the beam of the usherette's torch settled on us. We were slung out for being a nuisance.'

At St Thomas More's Lynn's closest friend was Kath Kavanagh (now married and called Meir). Kath remembers her as a girl who was bright and loved fun but just wouldn't knuckle down to work and was often in trouble with her teachers because of this attitude. Kath says:

There were a gang of us, and we thought of school as just being for fun. Lynn was naturally bright. She seemed to be able to get by without doing hardly any work. The nuns often had to rap her over the knuckles because of her japes. But it didn't make any difference. Nothing would make her take school seriously.

She says Lynn was good at art and English, and especially good at writing imaginative essays. On the sportsfield she starred at hockey and rounders.

Kath and Lynn occasionally got fed up with school and played truant. They would put their dinner money together and buy packets of ready-mixed curry. They would take them to Lynn's home, heat them up and spend the afternoon eating curry and listening to rock 'n' roll records.

Lynn loved music, and had a good singing voice. Kath recalls she had a rarer skill – she could yodel. 'She tried to teach me but I couldn't do it. But Lynn could yodel brilliantly,' she says.

A school report for the spring term of 1974 when Lynn was in the fourth form shows her attitude to education. She got an A for English, and was third in the class, the teacher commenting: 'Excellent result. Keep it up.' But in geography she got a D and the teacher wrote: 'Disgraceful effort. No revision.'

In most subjects she was 'satisfactory' or 'fair'. Her form teacher reported: 'Lynn is certainly not extending herself. She has the ability to achieve a better average in all subjects, especially such as history, geography, religious education and maths.'

But if she didn't show much enthusiasm for learning, she did for her out-of-school activities, especially dancing and listening to music. She loved rock 'n' roll, and she had a great sense of rhythm when she was bopping or jiving.

Kath says, 'We used to jive together, and whenever the music started, whether it was a group, a juke box or a record, Lynn and I would be first on the floor.'

She had lots of boyfriends, but no special one. Kath says, 'Sometimes the gang would head off to Markeaton Park with a group of boys. The boys liked Lynn because she was a toughie who gave as good as she got. If the boys punched her in fun or gave her a shove, she'd punch them back. She was very strong for a girl, and the boys respected this.'

But there was a feminine side to her as well. She was fond of dressing in smart clothes, making herself up nicely and looking good. She liked nice perfume. She and Kath tried to make perfume by soaking rose petals in water but it didn't work.

Whenever she went out at night, Lynn would always tell her grandmother where she was going, who she was going with, and what time she'd be home. But Flo still worried about her. She says, 'I always asked her to give me a yell when she reached the end of the Jitty to let me know she was all right.'

Another of her friends, Pat Broadhead (now Edmunds and living in Oakwood) remembers going up to The Greyhound with Lynn, and a group of friends for music sessions. Pat lived around the corner from Lynn in

Thackeray Street. She says, 'Lynn used to take a short cut through her garden to come to my place. She came so often she wore a hole in the hedge.'

After these sessions, they invariably stopped for a pea mix at the fish and chip shop on the way home. This was a portion of chips (no fish) topped with a portion of peas. Lynn used to eat prodigiously, especially junk food like crisps and nuts, but she never put on weight.

Lynn used to spend many hours around at Pat's house listening to records. She had built up a good collection of records herself. Her favourite was The King, Elvis Presley, but she also liked Billy Fury, The Seekers, Del Shannon and the Everly Brothers.

Pat remembers going to see a gypsy fortune teller with her in Derby Market Hall. The gypsy looked into her crystal ball and told her that if ever she did get married it would not be early in life. Lynn was delighted with this forecast. She said to Pat, 'Good. I'll be able to enjoy myself and have a really good time before settling down.'

But the fortune teller told her something else that did not please her – that she would shortly lose somebody close to her in the family. It was not long after that her grandfather, Fred, whom she adored, died suddenly of a heart attack.

If the fortune teller saw any threat to Lynn's own life in her crystal ball, she was not saying.

At this time Lynn did not know the people who had moved into the empty house at 27 Carlyle Street. Though they had been living there almost two years, Michael Brookes and his family had not met many of their neighbours. But that was soon to change.

6   Sex and Stabbing

The house in Carlyle Street was the first proper home the Brookes family had after Michael Brookes and Doris got married on 19 February 1965. Roy, her illegitimate son, was a 2-year-old toddler when they married. Roy's father was from Dominica.

For a while after the marriage they lived with Dot's parents in Derby where Mick, when he was working, drove a taxi. His own mother had re-married, and he didn't get on with his stepfather, John Paddy, who thought he was work-shy.

They drifted around various flats and houses and then they decided to move to Wales. At first they were happy, living first in Rhyl, then Abergele, but there were problems with Roy at school. He complained he was being picked on because of his colour, not just by other boys but by teachers as well.

On one occasion a teacher grabbed him by the hair and, according to fellow pupils, said, 'And as for this little monkey, he ought to get back to the trees where he belongs.'

Mick Brookes was furious when he heard about this and tried to report the teacher first to the police and then to the Race Relations Board. But the complaint got nowhere, and the police took no action.

Mick Brookes said later that this started a wave of persecution against the family. Eggs were thrown into their home through an open window. Slogans were painted on their door with words like 'Nigger go home'.

Drugs squad officers raided the house after receiving a report that Dot was smoking cannabis. The police called again after receiving a call that Mick was beating up his wife.

All of these reports Mick Brookes claims were without

foundation, and were made just to harass the family. It worked. After three troublesome years, they moved back to Derby.

At first they were put up in a hostel for the homeless. Some nights they had to sleep rough on benches at Normanton Park. Eventually they were given a house in Ely Street, but after three months they moved to Carlyle Street in Sinfin, a short walk from the Siddons neat home on the corner.

Mick Brookes was thirty-one when his family moved to Carlyle Street, Dot was a couple of years younger. Roy was thirteen and by this time their little girl Tracey, was five.

Outwardly, they were an ordinary family. Much of the time Mick Brookes was out of work, but so were many other men in Sinfin. Often there was no money in the house, and he would go out with his Alsatian dogs to try to catch a rabbit to feed the family. Their house, with peeling paint on the doors and windows, and grubby curtains, was the most dilapidated in the street.

But inside more sinister things were happening. The secrets of their bizarre sex life emerged in a statement Dot Brookes made later. She was talking about their marriage, and she said:

> It was only about two months after we were married that I realised Michael had rather strange ways. I realised he did not give me sexual satisfaction. He really only had sex for his own satisfaction.
>
> At first he used to get me to stand up against a wall in the house, at first when I was fully clothed, when he would prod my stomach with his thumb. He got me to lift up my clothes and he would masturbate himself. He asked me to masturbate him but I refused to do this.
>
> I got the impression that by going through the actions of prodding me he had some idea that he was stabbing me which gave him sexual satisfaction.
>
> Later on he would do this when I was naked or with very few clothes on. He never had sex with me when he did this.
>
> I was bothered about this, and because of this, and the fact that we did not have a very satisfactory sex relationship, I begged him to go and seek medical help. He refused to do this saying he would try to overcome it. He made no attempt to do this.

It was when I was pregnant that Michael seemed to do the prodding of my stomach all the more. Before my daughter was born, Michael did not go out with other women but when she was born Michael used to go to all night parties and I heard about other women. He still carried on the prodding me. He seemed to have always been interested in young women between 16 and 18 years of age.

It was after we had been married about two years that he would prod me with a knife. It was a small table knife at first, then a carving knife. He used to have a change of expression, he looked wild, and he used to get me to close my eyes because he said if I kept my eyes open it stopped him from concentrating.

This worried me quite a lot. This has been happening wherever we have been living and this has continued right up until the 3 April 1980 when Michael left home.

I used to see Michael stabbing pictures of nude women in a men's magazine, and women in underclothes in catalogues. I found a number of these magazines and catalogues in the bedroom behind the wardrobe and these were mutilated with stab wounds in the stomach of the people in the pictures. Also some of the photographs were slit down from the throat of the person and down through the stomach.

I challenged him about this and he said, 'It's none of your business. You should not be so fucking nosey.' He also said, 'As long as it's not you, you have nothing to worry about.'

When a film on Jack the Ripper came to Derby, Michael took me to see it and all through the film he was very excited and concentrated on it and he was looking wild, and he seemed to be living the whole thing through. He spoke about the film frequently after this. This seemed to make him do more of the prodding my body with knives.

He also went to see a film about cannibals, and he told me about how they killed a nurse or a nun and cut her up and ate the intestines. He lived this situation also.

On a number of occasions Michael would get me to lie across the bed with my head overhanging the side of the bed and with a knife in his hand he would be prodding me and he would be saying when he was stabbing me 'I am stabbing you and I am going to cut your head off ' but I realized this only satisfied his sexual desires.

None of the neighbours could have known of, or guessed at, the strange things that were happening behind those shabby curtains. Michael Brookes was a bit of a mystery in Sinfin. The local people knew nothing about his past – that he had twice tried to commit suicide, once by taking an overdose of tablets and another time by putting his head in a gas oven.

And they would not have known that he had spent some time in a mental hospital for treatment for his nerves after the second suicide attempt when he had phoned the police for help and they had persuaded him to go to Kingsway Hospital as a voluntary patient.

All the neighbours saw was rather a scruffy man with long arms and big feet loping around the pavements. He liked taking long walks and soon got to know all the tracks and footpaths around Sinfin.

The Brookes family did hardly any socializing, although they did welcome a succession of teenage girls to their home, including Lynn Siddons.

Lynn and her bestfriend, Pam Stocks, got to know the Brookes by accident. Pam had agreed to look after the twin babies of a woman who lived next door, Sheila Gunn. Lynn had said she would babysit with her. When the two girls knocked at Sheila's door, number 25, there was no reply. They found her next door with the Brookes.

The two girls became regular callers at the Brookes. But the main attraction was Dot. Pam recalls:

> She had a way of talking to us and making us feel grown up. She was good fun. We spent a lot of time playing cards with them, rummy – or snap if it was just a quick game. Sometimes Dot would cook up some outrageous meal – mixing a tin of chicken with mushroom soup or something like that. They were an unconventional family, and evenings with them were a bit of an adventure for two young girls.

Dot Brookes mentioned in her statement that Mick Brookes had a fondness for young girls. But Pam insists their evenings there were entirely innocent. She says, 'He never tried to touch us, or make any proposition or anything like that. Once he tickled Lynn but she told him to get away. But there was never anything sexual. Neither Lynn nor I liked him very much – it was Dot that we were friendly with.'

As well as playing cards, the two girls would listen to rock 'n' roll records, dancing to the loud music. Sometimes they would watch horror movies on TV. Once, after watching a late film, Mick Brookes offered to walk Lynn home. She didn't want him to because she didn't like him or trust him, and she asked Roy to walk her down the street instead.

Roy was friendly with Lynn, but he liked Pam even more. For a while she was his girlfriend. Her mother insisted the relationship should cease, and forbade Pam to visit the Brookes'. But she still continued to visit them surreptitiously, always with Lynn.

After she told Roy she no longer wanted to be his girlfriend, there was a curious incident one day at her school. She was called out to the school gates at lunchtime. Mick Brookes and Roy were there, and Mick handed her a letter.

It was written by him but signed by Roy, and it asked Pam if, when she was eighteen, she would agree to become engaged to Roy. The letter asked her to telephone Roy if she agreed. She tore the letter up and never made the call.

After thinking about it for many years, Pam cannot really explain this incident, other than that it may have been a ruse by Mick Brookes to keep her in with the family, so that she and the other teenage girls he liked to have around would keep coming to his house.

But Pam White is sure of one thing. She says: 'If it hadn't been Lynn who was murdered, I'm convinced I would have been the victim. The only purpose of this letter must have been to mark me down and make me available. I'm sure it would have been me if Lynn had somehow escaped their clutches.'

But Lynn did not escape. Mick Brookes had begun to plot her death well before 3 April, the day she was murdered. And she had only got to know the family and started visiting them two months before.

When Lynn went on the Italian holiday to see her godparents, she mentioned several times on the long train journey across France to both her mother and her grandmother that Roy Brookes had spoken to her about getting a job on a farm, and how she had agreed to go with him to look for work.

Back home, Brookes was probably relishing the thought

of plunging his knife into a real body instead of those pictures on his bedroom wall as Lynn, unaware of the fate that awaited her, went on those shopping trips to Milan to buy presents for him and his family.

As her grandmother said, 'She was a sweet kind girl. Whenever we went away, she'd always buy presents for her friends. At this time, unfortunately, she thought of the Brookes as her friends.'

A doll for Tracey, a double pack of playing cards for Roy, cigarettes for Dot and Mick – she tucked the little presents into her suitcase before starting the long journey home.

They didn't get back until late on the Saturday night. The next day they slept late. Flo got up to cook a Sunday dinner of roast lamb. Then Lynn went round to give the presents to her friends.

Even as she handed them over, Mick Brookes must have been refining his murder plan. As soon as she had gone, he said to Roy, 'You'd better have a look round those farms tomorrow to see if there's any work.'

Roy grudgingly agreed knowing exactly what Mick Brookes intended to do. The tender trap had been set – and Lynn's fate had been sealed.

Her funeral took place a fortnight after her body was found. As well as the family, more than 160 of her schoolfriends crowded into the church of St George and All Soldier Saints in Derby. Tears ran down their faces during the mass.

But there were no tears from Flo Siddons. She had done her crying earlier at the funeral parlour when she had found out she was to be denied a last look at Lynn, and a chance to say goodbye.

Flo had gone to the funeral parlour with Cynthia and Gail to see Lynn before the coffin lid was finally screwed down. But the undertaker had taken Cynthia gently by the arm.

'I wouldn't advise you to look at her,' he said. 'Just let us screw the lid down.'

'But why not?' asked Cynthia. 'My mum's come to say goodbye to her.'

The undertaker shook his head. 'Don't let her. Her face isn't a pretty sight. She was attacked by insects and animals while lying in the open. If your mum sees her, she'll have nightmares for the rest of her life. Just let us put the lid on, I beg you.'

Cynthia knew the advice was not only well meant, but sensible. So she agreed. And then she went to explain the situation to her mother.

Flo began to weep. Cynthia recalls, 'It was the only time in my life I've seen mum cry. She'd wanted to say goodbye to Lynn, and now she realised she couldn't. I went to comfort her but the old toughness returned ... "Get away. Stop fussing. I'll be all right".'

The funeral procession started from the Siddons' house in Carlyle Street. The undertaker, wearing his top hat, walked the length of the street in front of the cortege. At every house the families stood outside, heads bowed as the sad procession passed them.

But there was no one standing outside number 27, and the curtains were the only ones not drawn together in mourning. The windows were wide open, and loud rock music was blaring out as Lynn's body was borne away. There were no last respects from Michael Brookes for his victim.

After the funeral service, Lynn was cremated at Markeaton. Her schoolfriends presented the family with an inscribed vase. This marks the place at the cemetery in Melbourne where her ashes were buried next to those of her grandfather.

7 Wrong Man in the Dock

The trial of Fitzroy Patrick Joseph Brookes opened before Mr Justice Mais at the Shire Hall in Nottingham on Monday 6 November 1978, eight months after Lynn's body was found. The judge, the jury, the barristers in wigs and gowns, all peered curiously at the small pathetic figure in the dock charged with her murder.

He pleaded not guilty, even though the prosecuting barrister, Mr Graham Hamilton, QC, said he had twice made statements in which he had admitted stabbing Lynn. But as the trial progressed, it became obvious that even if Roy Brookes had a hand in the killing, he could not have done it alone.

One of the most important witnesses was Professor Alan Usher, the Home Office pathologist, who had examined Lynn's body which was lying on its back near the canal. There were bruises and scratches on her throat just above her Adam's apple, and more bruises on her sternum, or breastbone, and behind her ear which suggested her throat had been compressed either by a hand, hands or a forearm.

Then Dr Usher gave details of the stab wounds. Some of them were deep, the deepest, where the knife blade had penetrated four inches, in her lower pelvis. There were wounds in the lower abdomen, and underneath her left armpit were ten major stab wounds. There were other wounds on the loin, and the buttocks. These knife blows severed an artery to the kidney, perforated the lower bowel, liver and diaphragm.

But what intrigued the court were details Dr Usher gave of other wounds. Just above her navel were eleven tiny perforations caused, in his view, by just the tip of the knife being put into the skin.

He also found a long horizontal scratch in the left upper quarter of the abdomen which could have been caused by a knife blade being drawn across the skin.

This pattern of wounding tallied precisely with the account of Lynn's murder which Roy Brookes gave in his second statement – where he had been ordered by his stepfather to stick the knife in but, because he didn't want to hurt Lynn, had only done so gently. And the long horizontal scratch could have been left when he dragged the carving knife across her stomach deliberately breaking the blade from the handle.

Dr Usher gave the cause of Lynn's death as asphyxia due to compression of the neck, contributed to by shock and haemorrhage from multiple stab wounds. The stabbing, he said, could have been simultaneous with the strangulation.

He was asked by Mr Hamilton: You found that there was little blood present on the clothes or in the area?

A: Yes.
Q: How does that assist with finding of the cause of death?
A: Well, I feel this girl was dead or at the point of death when many of these stab wounds were inflicted.

Usher was cross-examined by Mr Douglas Draycott, QC, for the defence who asked him: She would be a girl, in ordinary circumstances, if she was approached by a chap to grab her, who would be capable of putting up some sort of a struggle, would she not?

A: Yes.
Q: And the indications here are that she did not get much of an opportunity?
A: Precisely.

Another witness was Detective Inspector Arthur Padmore who spoke of the early interviews with Roy Brookes when he had claimed Lynn had just disappeared but after the discovery of her body he eventually admitted stabbing her when she called him a 'stupid black bastard'.

At first, he said that Lynn did nothing with her clothing before the stabbing, but after having a short discussion with his stepfather, he told police she had lifted her upper clothing and asked him to touch her.

He declined, and she began calling him names so he stuck the knife into her. She started screaming, so he knifed her again.

The knife was about seven to eight inches long, he said. He thought he stabbed her about four times and then the knife broke. He became frightened and ran off, throwing the blade into the canal.

Detective Inspector Padmore said the stepfather was in custody for about forty-eight hours in connection with the offence. Then he was released on bail. But he was not bailed currently, and had not been charged.

This, of course, was the case for the prosecution. Only Roy Brookes was in the dock. Only one person had been charged with Lynn's murder. As the trial progressed, more and more people in the courtroom were becoming convinced the wrong person had been charged.

The second statement by Roy named his stepfather as the killer. Though the youth hesitated once or twice and seemed occasionally to be at a loss for the right word, the main track of his story as he told it in court never wavered from the version he had told to his solicitor and Dr Dorman in Leicester Jail. Those who heard it felt it was the truth more especially because of the way it matched up to the forensic evidence.

The same cannot be said of the story Michael Brookes produced to account for his whereabouts at the time of the killing. He had gone into the witness box to give evidence against Roy, but soon he was shuffling uneasily as relentless probing ripped his alibi into shreds.

Describing his own movements on the afternoon of Lynn's death, he said he had walked through the Rolls Royce car park and along the field towards Red Wood. There he had met Roy. He had asked him where Lynn was, and Roy had replied she had gone off when he went into the trees to the toilet.

When he was cross-examined by Mr Draycott, the difficult questions started coming thick and fast:

Q: I do not want you to be under any misunderstanding. I am suggesting to you that you were a party to this killing and indeed played a principal part. Do you understand?

A: Yes, sir.

Q: You have in fact been arrested for this offence, have you not?

A: Yes, they did come to arrest me. Yes sir.

Q: Did you make any admission of any sort during the interviews the police had with you?

A: No sir.

Q: Of course, you know that your son has made two statements?

A: Yes, I believe so, sir.

Q: Have you read those statements or either of them?

A: No sir.

Q: The police put to you in detail the contents of the second statement that had been made shortly before your arrest, did they not?

A: I am sorry?

Q: The police put to you in detail the contents of the second statement your son had made?

A: A few details.

Q: They put to you the substance, did they not, of what he was saying and a history of an association with you that involved threats to kill women?

A: That is ridiculous.

Q: A long association where you both went out on walks and had a knife or knives.

A: No, sir.

Q: But that was suggested to you?

A: Yes, sir.

Q: They also told you that he told them that you stuck knives into pictures of women?

A: They did, sir.

Q: And to cut a story quite short, that at the time of the killing, it was you who held the girl from behind and strangled her?

A: I was not even there.

Q: But that was put to you?

A: Yes, that is what they said to me. Yes sir.

Q: You understood, did you not, that there was no independent evidence to implicate either him or you?

A: Yes, that is right sir.

Q: Except, of course, in the boy's case, a confession, and you did not make a confession?

A: No, sir.

Q: You say there is no truth in any of this?

A: No, sir.

He was next asked about the walk he claimed to have taken with Roy the day before Lynn's death when, he said, he had spoken to a man sitting on a wall about getting work for the boy. Mr Draycott asked him which farm it was. He didn't know the name of it. Then he was asked to point it out on the map. He couldn't, even though he said he regularly walked around the fields and around the farms. Next Brookes was asked why he hadn't taken Roy back to the farm on the Monday.

Q: Why did you not take him? He is a boy who cannot read or write, I understand?

A: Well, I had other problems to sort out.

Q: What problems did you have to sort out?

A: Well, very very private ones.

Q: However private they are, you must tell us about them. What was it that made you not do the obvious, which was to walk along with Roy to this farm?

A: Well, for weeks we had a lot of trouble. Not too bad, but the wife had always gone or got on at me to do something about it because my family was not speaking and we was.... Well, in our opinion, Roy was shoved on one side and I had to approach my mother to try and sort things out.

Q: Families often have troubles. Was it anything out of the ordinary?

A: Yes, we think so.

Q: Why did you not do something about it on the Sunday then instead of wandering around the fields with Roy if it was that pressing?

A: Because the sort of problems we had got it was always best if I went up and my stepfather was not in – Mr Paddy.

Q: The contrast I am seeking to draw here is that you have got a boy who has been trying to get a job. You have got an opportunity to get him a job yet you say you did not go off with him. You send him off on his own with a girl. Why did you not go with him? That is what I am asking you. What was so pressing on this 3rd April that made you not do what I suggest any father would have done who had nothing better to do?

A: Normally it is always a Monday that I go or could always get to see my mother. It was either in the morning, or sometimes when Mr Paddy used to come home, he used to come home at dinner time. It was either a chance when I called up in the morning to see her or in the afternoon.

Brookes' testimony about the visit he claimed to have made to his mother came under unremitting scrutiny. This was his alibi – the place he said he had been visiting, and the reason for the visit, at the time Lynn was being killed.

Q: You decided on Monday morning to go and see your mother?
A: Yes, for weeks well the wife's been going on about it. On this Monday morning, I got up and the wife and me had a bit of a dust up about it.
Q: Can you put it in a few short words what the dust up was about?
A: Well I suppose about me being unemployed and not in work and sort of degraded.
Q: You?
A: I was not up to my family standards.
Q: What has this to do with Roy?
Q: Well, my family was against me marrying my wife and taking on Roy.
Q: How long have you been married at this stage on the 3rd April?
A: Thirteen years.
Q: And you say all this comes to a head on the morning of the 3rd April when you decide to go up and see your mother because Mr Paddy you think will be out?
A: Yes sir.

Tension mounted in the courtroom as the questions went on, each producing answers that seemed to get more and more ludicrous. Brookes shuffled and twitched as the quizzing continued.

He had chosen to go on the Monday morning, he said, because Monday was his mother's washing day, and he could be reasonably sure she would be in.

Q: Let us take it by stages. This was in the morning you decide to go up, is it?
A: Yes, in the morning.
Q: And you went up, did you?
A: No, I did not call in.

Q: I did not ask you that. I said did you go to your mother's
house?
A: No, sir.
Q: What did you do?
A: I went to sign on.
Q: Where did you go to sign on?
A: The unemployment exchange in Derby.
Q: Does that take you past your mother's house?
A: It does.
Q: Both going and coming back from signing on?
A: Yes sir.
Q: There you are, and what did your mother have to say
about all this?

Before Brookes answered, Mr Justice Mais announced
the court would adjourn for lunch. And he did something
else which is extremely rare in court procedure. He ordered
that Brookes should not be allowed to wander about during
the lunch adjournment.

Brookes was not in the dock. He was the chief prosecution
witness. But the judge asked for the police to make
arrangements to provide him with food saying, 'I just do not
think it is right that he should be on the free.'

8   Crumbling Alibi

If he had felt uncomfortable under the barrage of tricky questions during the morning session, Michael Brookes was to face worse in the afternoon. Slowly Mr Draycott extracted a story from him that was unbelievable in its stupidity.

For those with a taste for courtroom drama, it is repeated here verbatim as a perfect example of skilful alibi demolition.

Q: Mr Brookes, we had reached this stage that on this Monday, 3rd April, and because of some family disturbance concerning you taking on Roy when you married your wife, it was necessary for you to go and see your mother. You told us that you went to sign on in the morning and that route would take you past your mother's house?

A: Yes.

Q: What did you do about it?

A: What do you mean? When I went up to sign on or...

Q: When you approached your mother's front door you passed it?

A: Yes, I did pass it.

Q: When you passed your mother's front door going along the street, what did you do about it?

A: I looked through the front room window. It was directly on the pavement sort of thing and carried on then down to sign on.

Q: Pause there. You looked through the front room window?

A: In the front window.

Q: You have told us that this is normally washday. She does not do her washing in the front room, does she?

A: No, but she often goes in the front.

Q: She may often go in the front, but this is Monday morning washday. Do you expect her to be in the front room on the Monday morning washday?

A: No, I have explained the reason why I did not go round the back.

Q: What is the reason you did not go round the back?

A: Because sometimes my stepfather Mr Paddy has days off. My mother had had explicit instructions that if I did call in that I was not to go in. I used to have to go up there to find out if he was in and if she was in.

Q: That is what I understood you to be saying. I want you to tell the jury how you found out if she was in or was not in?

A: I did not know until early in the afternoon when I went up.

Q: Do not go on. Deal with the morning. On your way to the labour exchange what steps do you say you took to find out whether your mother was in or out?

A: Well, I did not.

Q: You did not?

A: No, because that morning I was rather late and on Monday I never had any money to go on the bus.

Q: Wait a minute. You were rather late. You mean late to sign on?

A: No, well, normally I have the money to go on the bus. I would normally catch the ten past eleven bus. If I did not, I would perhaps leave about quarter to eleven, something like that.

Q: What are you late for?

A: I am sorry?

Q: The only duty you have, as I see it, in the morning is to sign on?

A: Yes, sir.

Q: What time did you sign on?

A: I signed on at quarter to twelve. Well, ten to twelve, and my official time is quarter to.

Mr Justice Mais then put a question. 'But you were not late for that. What were you late for, you have been asked?'

A: Well, I was not late.

Again the judge: You were late for something. What were you late for?

A: Well, there was a queue and I signed on.

Again Mr Draycott took up the questioning:

Q: But you did not know that at the time you were outside your mother's house. If there is any substance in this, it is not for me, but it is a matter for the jury to decide. But it seems to be absurd that a grown man .... How old are you?

A: Thirty-three.

Q: Yes, thirty-three. Because of some row, you go up to see your mother. When you get there, you say you do not do anything except look through the window. Is that right?

A: That is correct.

Q: And the reason you say you do not do anything then is because you say that you were late?

A: No. What I meant is I had not got time to go round.

Q: That is the same thing, So you go to the labour exchange and you sign on?

A: Yes.

Q: What is your problem then on the way back?

A: I walked back home. I was in two minds to call in again, but I would not dare call in because when I got back up there it is about twenty past twelve, half past twelve, and obviously Mr Paddy would be in.

Q: What time do you say you signed on?

A: Quarter to twelve.

Q: You thought he would be in?

A: Yes, because he comes home for dinner.

Q: You did not knock on the door or anything?

A: No.

Q: I mean he is not going to bite you. You have only to knock on the door to see if your mother is in?

A: No, I have been married for 13 years to my wife and I have never in that 13 years not really ever got on with none of my family.

Q: What on earth is causing the hurry in your mind then on this 3rd April that makes it necessary to go up and air a problem that you say has existed for 13 years?

A: Yes, because on a Monday normally is the day when I call up normally on the way to the employment exchange. Sometimes when my mother and me were talking I would go up on a Monday morning and I would go on in and my mam would give me a cup of tea in the kitchen and she was always saying, 'Try and make sure you come when John is not in.'

Q: Every Monday morning it was your practice to drop in and see your mother and have a cup of tea, was it not?

A: If I did not call in the morning, I would sometimes call in the afternoon or any other day I could get up.

Q: You see, Mr Brookes, let us face it. If there is any truth in what Roy is saying, you have to provide yourself with some sort of an alibi for the afternoon, half past one to half past three, have you not?

A: Yes, sir.

Q: Because either you were at the scene of the killing as he said or you were elsewhere?

A: I have told you, when I made the statement to the police. I told them where I went and that is exactly where I did go. I left my house. I went up to my mother's. I went round the back. There was nobody in. I came away and I went walking round Sinfin.

Q: You had been twice past your mother's house in the morning. Correct?

A: Yes.

Q: Contrary to your usual practice, you say you had not called in and had a cup of tea. Correct?

A: Yes.

Q: So this is the reason you go for another time, a third time?

A: No reply.

Q: In the afternoon?

A: There is many a day that I have gone up, left my home to go to my mother's and even my wife has been with me at times but I have got to the house and we have never bothered going in.

Q: Just deal with this 3rd April. The reason you are giving for going up in the afternoon is that you had not seen your mother as you wanted to in the morning?

A: No. One of the main reasons that I got to get something sorted out. Two weeks I think it was prior to this I went on a Wednesday afternoon to play bingo with my wife and my mother was in the bingo with somebody – Mr Paddy – and neither of us spoke. We never just got on. After that my wife was on about it because at this time the Electricity Board had disconnected us for a bill for £25.00 and my wife wanted me to keep going up and asking my family for help to have it put back on.

Q: One more reason for going in when you were there that Monday morning then?

A: No reply.

Q: If it is not Roy but the Electricity Board that is the trouble, why not go in when you have every reason to think, because of your past experience, that your mother will be on her own? If it is not too private a reason for going up in the afternoon?

A: No reply.

Q: Let us test it. Did you see your mother in the afternoon? Can she corroborate it?

A: No, my mother was not in.

Q: No?

A: No.

Q: No?

A: I never. She was not in on that Monday.

Q: Is it right that she was not in in the afternoon?

A: Well, I did not see her in.

Q: That is not the same thing. Are you drawing a distinction between her not being in and you not seeing her in?

A: I went ... There is a bit of a jitty. It went up the back.

Q: Are you drawing a distinction between knowing your mother was not in or simply saying that you did not see her in?

A: Well, I did not see her in.

Q: Did you knock at the door?

A: No.

Q: Let us get this right. What do you say you did do?

A: I just went round the back and stood at the gate. I did not go in because I have told you before sometimes Mr Paddy does not go to work in the afternoon.

Q: Mr Brookes, this is very important. You are now saying that on your third trip past that house, or to that house, you still did not knock at the door and see your mother?

A: No, because if I had knocked at the door and Mr Paddy would have been in we would have probably ended up coming to fighting.

Q: Have you ever fought with him before?

A: Yes, on one occasion.

Q: When was that?

A: That was....

Q: How long ago?

A: Eight years.

Q: Eight years?

A: As far as I can recollect.

Q: Mr Brookes, does it not strike you as implausible?

A: I am sorry?

Q: Does this not strike you as nonsense?

A: No reply.

Q: That a grown man who wants to see his mother goes to

the house, or the vicinity of the house, for the third time, you say, in the afternoon and you do not bother to find out if she is in?

A: I have explained why.

Q: What was the reason why? That your stepfather might be in?

A: I thought Mr Paddy would be in the house.

Q: Then why go at all?

A: Because I went to try to see my mother. I think to understand that position you have to be in the position.

Q: Well, I'm doing my best. I certainly understand what you are saying. What you are saying is this, is it not, that you did not make any attempt to see your mother because you thought Mr Paddy might be in the house?

A: Yes, because it....

Q: Never mind why for the moment. Then what on earth is the purpose of going up to the house in the afternoon?

A: Because if Mr Paddy was not in and my mam was in I would have probably been all right. I would have knocked and gone in.

Q: Then how do you resolve the problem when you get there to see if Mr Paddy is in or not? You can only do it by knocking and saying 'Can I come in?' Is that right?

A: Well, let us just put it another way. I suppose that I just have not got the guts to face him because of trouble.

Q: But you were making a special journey according to you?

A: I am often going up to try to see my mam.

Q: No. No. Your practice is to see your mum on your Monday mornings and have a cup of tea. You are saying on the afternoon of the killing you made a special journey to see your mother, yet made no attempt to see her when you got there. That is what it amounts to, is it not?

A: Yes, and my answer to you for that question was that when I went up there I was not sure if Mr Paddy was in.

Q: But what is the difference between the situation when you left your house to go up there and when you got there? If you ever did.

A: Well, I was up there.

Q: What is the difference between the situation as you knew it when you left your house at about twenty past one and when you got up to your mother's house? It is exactly the same as far as Mr Paddy is concerned. You do not know whether he is in or not?

A: No reply.

Q: Do you understand?

A: No reply.

Q: You see you are putting yourself at the material time on a journey up to your mother's, are you not?

A: Yes, sir.

Q: Which takes what – a quarter-of-an-hour?

A: It is about a 20 minute walk.

Q: Well, a quarter-of-an-hour or 20 minutes. We have got evidence, and it will be heard, that it is about a quarter-of-an-hour normal walking. You are a fit chap, are you not?

A: Yes.

Q: Yes?

A: Then I suppose it depends on how fast you walk, does it not?

Q: Of course it does. But you are a fit man. You are used to walking for 15–20 minutes?

A: Yes.

Q: It is 15 minutes ordinary walking there and 15 minutes ordinary walking back. Where were you between 1.20 and 3.30?

A: Well, when I left the house at twenty past one I walked up to my mother's. I walked up to the Barracks on St Thomas Road where my mother lives. I walked round the back and I stood at the gates.

Q: Stood at the back gate?

A: Yes. There is a passageway that leads off the road and the gate is on the left hand side if you are walking up. I stood at the back window.

Q: How is it going to help you if you see your mother through the window? That will not help you to see if Mr Paddy is in?

A: Well, normally, if she sees me, I will wave or she waves.

Q: How long did you stay, do you say, in this sort of position?

A: I was there ... I do not know. About five minutes.

Q: It would not be longer, would it?

A: No. Then I went round to the front of the house and looked in there. I was there a few minutes.

Q: Any sign of your mother's washing?

A: To be quite honest, I didn't even look. I cannot remember.

The cross-examination went on, but Michael Brookes' alibi was in tatters. And he could have saved himself that last journey to his mother's house, if, as he claimed, he desperately needed to see her, by making a phone call.

Mr Draycott asked him if he remembered her number and he recalled it – 25133. But when questioned why, if he didn't want a confrontation with his stepfather, he hadn't simply dialled the number and asked 'Is it all right to come round?' he replied, 'I do not know.'

But it is believed that he did dial the number. When there was no reply, he thought to himself, 'Right, here's my alibi. I can say I went up to my mother's, and she wasn't in.'

And off he walked with his long loping stride to keep his appointment with murder on the banks of the canal.

9 Vengeance shall be Ours!

By the time Michael Brookes had finished giving his testimony, just about everybody in that tense courtroom knew that Roy Brookes, if not entirely innocent, was less guilty than his stepfather.

Most of the Siddons family had been in court every day of the four-day trial. They had always suspected Michael Brookes was behind Lynn's death, and what they had heard in court seemed to bear out this suspicion.

They, like others, must have had a nagging doubt about why Roy, simple-minded though he was, should have made that first confession that resulted in him alone facing the charge for Lynn's murder.

The answer came in Douglas Draycott's piercing cross-examination when he was questioning Michael Brookes about those vital ten minutes he had spent alone with Roy at Pear Tree police station the night he was arrested.

The two policemen who were questioning Roy about the killing couldn't get anything out of him. Michael Brookes was left alone with him while the detectives retired. When they returned, Roy began to talk. But first he had said, 'Can Dad tell you what happened?'

Michael Brookes prevaricated in the witness box, though he was asked four times why Roy should have used those words. It was suggested to him that he knew just what had happened, and would explain it better to the two detectives. He was not able to give a satisfactory answer.

The suggestion was put to him that during those ten minutes he reminded Roy to stick to the story they had concocted where Roy would take the entire blame for the killing. After all, he, a minor, would only get a few years in a remand home if found guilty, whereas Michael Brookes would almost certainly get a life sentence – and not be too popular with his fellow prisoners who tend to give those responsible for killing young girls a hard time.

Michael Brookes said this was ridiculous. But then, as Flo Siddons said later, he would, wouldn't he?

The final speeches by counsel for the prosecution and defence were to a jury that must have pretty well made up its mind.

Graham Hamilton, prosecuting, put the question, 'Even if one accepts that the boy told the truth in his last long statement to the police, is one not compelled to come to the conclusion that he took an active part in the lethal assault?'

Mr Hamilton raised another point on the claim that Roy Brookes played his role in the killing under duress because of his father's threat to kill his mother.

He said, 'In the past he has never done what his father wanted. But his father had never attempted to get his mum.'

Mr Draycott pointed out that the wounds to Lynn's body as outlined by the pathologist tallied with the boy's account of his part in the attack.

He said, 'Where you have that sort of support for the boy's account, it would be utterly unsafe to disregard it.'

He also said that Dr Usher had put forward the view that the murder seemed to have been committed by somebody in a mad sexual frenzy. Yet there had been evidence from Mrs Siddons, the girl's grandmother, that Lynn and Roy were just friends with no sexual relationship.

Mr Justice Mais, in his summing up, took up a point that had been made several times throughout the trial – the stature of the accused boy as compared with Lynn who was taller, heavier and more powerful. The judge said:

> You may not think this was a one-man or a one-boy job. At any rate, you may think it was not a one-boy job. If this accused was there and then present, assisting the other in some way, he could be equally guilty of murder if he knew there was the intention to kill or to cause really serious bodily harm, if in fact it was a joint enterprise to kill or cause really serious bodily harm. But he would not be guilty even if he was there unless you were convinced that he knew of the

intention to kill or to do really serious bodily harm to this girl.

The judge reminded the jury of the long cross-examination of Michael Brookes on his alibi. The point was to demonstrate he could not account for his movements that afternoon for an hour or so up to the time of 3.20 p.m. when, according to him, he met Roy returning alone from his walk.

Another point the judge highlighted was the dragging of Lynn's body into the deepest and thickest part of the undergrowth. Tests had been carried out with various weights which had shown it to be almost impossible for a weakling like Roy Brookes to have dragged the body to where it was found.

He went on, 'Now there is evidence which, if you would believe it, would demonstrate that the accused's stepfather, Michael Richard Brookes, was an accomplice.' The judge explained the difficulties of accepting evidence of an accomplice without corroboration, and he reminded the jury, 'The stepfather is not being tried before you.'

During his lengthy summing up, the judge made this point more than once. It was a necessary reminder. Some of those jurors, if they had allowed their minds to wander, must have felt, as did others in the courtroom, that it was Michael Brookes who was being tried, not Roy.

Before they retired, the judge told the jury:

You may well think there may have been someone else there, and this could not have been done by this boy alone, and, as I say, you may think this makes sense particularly if you accept the evidence of Dr Usher that the cause of death was asphyxia due to compression of the neck and the death was contributed to by shock and multiple stab wounds.

Because you may recall the evidence that there was very little blood about, and these wounds were caused at the time of death, or just before or just after the point of death, and you ask yourselves when you retire, as no doubt you will, was this young man capable of asphyxiating Lynn, when you bear in mind what her physique was, and so on. And, as I say, if you were satisfied there was someone else there, then the original statements to the police obviously are completely and utterly untrue.

The jury took just twenty minutes to reach their unanimous verdict that Roy Brookes was not guilty. The judge told them he agreed with their verdict.

And so did Flo Siddons. She and Gail had followed the evidence closely. They knew that Roy Brookes couldn't have murdered Lynn by himself, even if he had taken a minor role in the killing. The man they wanted to see in the dock was Michael Brookes.

Flo recalls, 'We thought the judge would order his arrest, or the police would take him away immediately the trial ended. We were amazed when he was allowed to go free when nearly all the evidence we'd heard pointed to him as the killer.'

The judge ordered that Roy Brookes, even though found not guilty, should be taken to a place of safety for his own protection. But Michael Brookes was allowed to return to his home.

If he felt relieved, he didn't show it. There was an air of arrogance about him when he faced reporters outside the court and parried their questions.

He told a reporter from the *Sun*, 'I know the jury's decision points to me as the guilty man. I don't give a hoot if tongues may wag. I know I was not there when the girl was killed, and I didn't plan it. There may have been another person there as well as Roy but it certainly wasn't me.'

Even Michael Brookes' mother, Mrs Paddy – the mother he claimed in court he had gone to see at the vital time of the killing – expected him to be arrested. She steadfastly believed in his innocence, but after the trial she said, 'I only wish the whole wretched business could have ended, but now there is talk of my son being arrested and the whole thing is looming over us like a big, dark cloud.'

Back in Sinfin, the Siddons family felt relieved that the trial was over, but disappointed that Michael Brookes had not been immediately arrested. Flo brewed a pot of tea and as she handed cups to Gail and Cynthia, they consoled themselves with the thought that the law, even if a little tardy, must soon catch up with him.

As Flo said, 'Even the judge had pointed out that Roy Brookes couldn't have done the killing alone. There must have been somebody else with him – and who could it be if it wasn't Mick Brookes.'

Behind the faded curtains at number 27, Mick and Dot contemplated their future. They didn't dare wander out and risk meeting the hostility of their neighbours.

Michael Brookes gave an interview to a local newspaper. He said, 'I have been made a scapegoat. I am being victimized. I have only been out once in the last four days because of threats made against me and my family.

'I had nothing to do with Lynn's murder. Not one of these allegations can be proved. I don't honestly know why Roy made these allegations, but it sounds to me as if something has been put into the lad's head.'

Dot Brookes also gave vent to her feelings:

Nobody knows what we have gone through with this. I feel sorry for Mrs Siddons – Lynn was like a daughter to me. But no matter what I say or what I do, I cannot bring that girl back.

For crying out loud, let them get the right man, not jump to conclusions. We just want to be left in peace.

Their reported statements made it appear as if both Mick Brookes and his wife would like to get to the truth so that his name would be cleared and his wife's wish to live in peace would be granted.

But they turned down one opportunity. Psychiatrists who had been studying Roy's behaviour wanted to give him an injection of the truth drug to see which version of Lynn's killing he would then give – that he had done it alone, or merely assisted his stepfather.

But Michael Brookes and Dot both said no very firmly to this suggestion, Brookes giving as his reason that he had no faith in the medical profession.

Every month, Flo Siddons goes to visit the cemetery at Melbourne where Lynn's ashes are buried beside those of her grandfather who died of a sudden heart attack just three months before Lynn was murdered. Sometimes she goes with Gail, sometimes with Cynthia, sometimes all three of them go.

They always take a bunch of flowers which they put in the vase Lynn's schoolfriends bought and gave to the family.

It became obvious in the weeks following the trial that Michael Brookes was not going to be arrested. The police claimed they hadn't got the evidence to charge him. Having charged the wrong person in the first place, they were now in a dilemma about charging the right person.

The anguish of the Siddons family grew. They couldn't bear to see Lynn's killer free. Flo Siddons says, 'If I saw him in the street, waves of hatred came over me. If I had had a chance, I would have killed him myself.'

One Sunday a month or so after the trial, Flo went on her pilgrimage to the cemetery at Melbourne. Gail and Cynthia were with her.

The three tiny women stood looking sadly at the memorial. There and then they made a vow that they would avenge her death by bringing her killers to justice. No matter how long it took or what difficulties lay in the way, they were determined Michael Brookes would pay the price for his actions.

10 Family Loyalty

The little village of Melbourne, eight miles south of Derby, was chosen for Lynn Siddons' burial because it was the birthplace of her grandmother, Florence Siddons. It's a very old village, mentioned in the Domesday Book as Mileburne (Mill by the Stream).

History touched it briefly a couple of times. It was the southernmost point reached by Bonnie Prince Charlie and his army in 1745. Half a century later, the Lamb family who lived at Melbourne Hall produced William Lamb who, as the second Viscount Melbourne, became Prime Minister to Queen Victoria.

Lord Melbourne gave his name to a cluster of houses on the banks of the River Yarra in Australia. They grew, of course, to become Australia's second city. His wife was also well known – but for different reasons. Lady Caroline Lamb's affair with the poet Byron was the first of many which scandalized society and brought about their much-publicized separation.

But these momentous happenings did not impinge on village life which went on as it had down the centuries. The main relief from the daily drudge of hard toil on the land was the annual fair where the youths and girls assembled in the market place to hire themselves to the farmers and landowners. Once they were paid their 'hiring shilling', they were decked with a ribbon to show they were no longer available.

Then the workers went back to their labours in the market gardens, weaving mills and shoe factories, bringing up their offspring in the well-worn groove of hard work, Sunday worship and 'looking after your own'.

This way of life produced a fierce family loyalty, and it was into this tradition that Florence Siddons was born on 15 November 1914 as the shells were bursting over Europe after the outbreak of the First World War. Her father, William Barradell, worked in the weaving trade and walked along the dusty lanes from Derby to court her mother, Sarah.

They had married earlier that year and by the time Flo was born (in the cottage where Thomas Cook, founder of the travel agency, once lived) William Barradell was away in France driving a lorry with food and supplies to the men at the front. He was one of the first of the men from Melbourne to volunteer. Sarah didn't see her husband again, nor Flo her father, until the war was over in 1918 and he and his comrades came marching back to the village.

They had been away a long time, and many of their friends had been killed. The little band of soldiers didn't go straight to their homes. After their long march, they stopped for a drink at the White Swan in Potter Street.

Flo, not yet five years old, remembers the soldiers piling their kit bags outside the pub. She hardly knew her father – he had picked her up and kissed her – but she undid his kit bag and rummaged inside. There was bound to be a present for her. Yes, there was. A pretty doll. She clutched it and ran off squealing with joy.

Her mother was a Roman Catholic, and she persuaded William to become a convert. Every Sunday little Flo would put on her best dress and go to mass.

When William came out of the army, he found he could make a better living than weaving using his new skill of driving. He drove a milk lorry from the depot at Shelton Lock to Loughborough, and sometimes he took his little girl in the cab with him as a special treat.

The family lived in Pingle Cottages, squeezing into a home with one living room, a tiny kitchen, and one bedroom divided into two. Flo had the luxury of her own bed until her two brothers came along. Then the three of them slept together.

Her mother, Sarah, got a job stitching up shoes at the local factory, Wilson's, which, for some forgotten reason, everyone called Sausages. After she left school at fourteen, Flo also worked at a shoe factory, Loakes.

She earned nine shillings a week for working from six o'clock in the morning to six in the evening. She and five other girls stood around a bench tying shoes in pairs. There was a half-hour stop for breakfast, and a half-hour stop for lunch, and if the woman in charge caught any of the girls sneaking a nibble at their sandwiches in between the official stops, there was trouble.

The family were not the poorest in the village, but they were not the richest, either. Flo remembers always having plenty to eat in her younger days, and having nice clothes. But she had to work hard for these things. Her mother and father always worked hard, and the children were brought up believing that only through hard work could they enjoy the rewards of life.

William Barradell was a strict but kind father. Like many Derbyshire fathers, and indeed fathers in other parts of the country, one of his great fears was of his daughter getting into trouble. Flo was forbidden to stay out late at night, and whenever she had a tryst with a boyfriend, her father would always be lurking around in the background.

She recalls, 'When I was fifteen, I had met this boy. We hadn't got any money, so we couldn't go anywhere. We were just holding hands by the warm forge in the blacksmith's shop. My father burst in and told me to get off home.'

This upbringing, strict but kind, was to forge those strong family bonds that would sustain Flo in her later life as she waged her campaign to bring Lynn's killers to justice. The ethic that you look after your own had been bred into her, and fighting her long battle on behalf of Lynn was something, as she says, she just had to do. It was a natural instinct, like a mother hen protecting her brood. But life wasn't all serious for young Flo. She was christened Florence, but she has always been a Flo. There was a cinema and a dance hall in Melbourne, but mostly the teenagers made their own fun. Carnival day was a big occasion, and Flo recalls making a grass skirt and, with half-a-dozen of her friends, entering the fancy dress competition as Hawaiian slave girls.

'We paraded through the main street on a lorry and had great fun,' she says. They won first prize – but she lost her boyfriend. 'He didn't like me flaunting my figure for every-body to see.'

Soon Flo changed her job and started work at the Co-op shoe factory in Abbey Street, Derby. It meant an eight-mile cycle ride to get to work, and again to get home, but this was nothing to a fit young girl. Sometimes, after cycling sixteen miles in the day, she and her friends would catch a bus to Swadlincote to go to the dance at Swad Rink. After dancing all evening, the gang of girls would walk the nine miles to get back home.

It was while cycling to work that she met her husband. Fred Siddons, a good-looking young man, was working on a building site at Shelton Lock which Flo passed every morning and every evening.

She says, 'I saw this man looking at me. Then he began to wave and smile. I couldn't help noticing him – he'd got lovely flashing white teeth. I pulled up on my bike and we had a chat. He arranged to come out to Melbourne the next evening and take me for a walk. It was a lovely sunny evening and we walked around the old windmill which used to be in the fields nearby.'

The gentle romance blossomed into love, and Fred and Flo were married in 1936 at St Phillipa's Roman Catholic Church in Melbourne. Because the Co-op did not employ married women, Flo had to give up her job. But she got a part-time job at Sausages, the same place as her mother, making army boots.

Keith, the eldest of her four children, was born in 1939 and Barrie a year later. But just as the First World War had disrupted the early years of her mother's marriage, the Second World War was to separate Fred and Flo.

Because he was involved in essential building work, Fred managed to defer his call up for a year or two. But then he was ordered to report to barracks at Sheringham in Norfolk. Flo managed to visit him once or twice but then Fred was sent home on embarkation leave before being posted to a fighting unit abroad.

The family had lived in several homes around Derby but in 1940, just before Barrie was born, they were allocated a council house in Sinfin. All the streets on the new estate were named after writers or poets – there was Shakespeare Street and Thackeray Street, Shelley Drive and Wordsworth Drive.

The house that Flo and her husband moved into was number 1 Carlyle Street. It was to be their home for the next forty years – up to the time of Fred's sudden death from a heart attack, and, three months later, Lynn's murder.

Flo showed a flash of that flinty Derbyshire stubbornness when Fred's embarkation leave came to an end and it was time for him to rejoin his regiment.

'I don't want you to go,' she said.

'I don't want to go – but I must,' Fred replied.

But there was a warmth in that house with his two little sons and attractive young wife that Fred Siddons just couldn't bear to leave. He decided to stay for one more night, then another, and, realizing that he was absent without leave, several more nights.

After a week, a policeman and a military policeman came looking for the absentee. Flo told him to go upstairs and hide in the loft, and she shooed the two little boys to play outside in the rainy backyard so they wouldn't say anything about their dad to give the game away.

They didn't find Fred, and they went away. But after another night, he knew he would be in serious trouble if he stayed at home, so he went to the police station and gave himself up. The Army soon forgave this little aberration. They promoted him to sergeant.

Fred went off with his regiment to Italy. He fought at Anzio and took part in the famous battle of Monte Casino where the Allies bombarded the fortified monastery south of Rome for days before it fell. Flo has a photograph of her husband marching proudly through Rome after the city was captured.

Flo found herself expecting again – as she says, 'I got caught with Gail on that last leave.' She wrote to Fred telling him, and he was wildly excited. After two boys, he had badly wanted a girl and even wrote letters with ideas for names. They were always girls' names he suggested, never boys, and Irene Gail had already been chosen when the baby girl was born on 4 October 1944.

Gail was eighteen months old when her dad came back from the war. Her mother had proudly shown the tiny girl pictures of her father in uniform, so she knew what he looked like. When he got home he couldn't wait to see his daughter. He picked her up and hugged her and cuddled her and couldn't bear to leave her.

He had plenty of time to be with her. Jobs were hard to come by, and it was a year or more before he was able to get work back in the building trade. He spent much of this time playing with Gail, taking her for walks, teaching her to tell the time, and to read children's books.

It was in February 1946 that Fred got home, and by the end of the year Flo had given birth again. It was another girl, Cynthia, born on 29 November.

The family was now complete – two boys, and two girls. Flo continued working at the Co-op shoe factory. They needed her wage packet until Fred was able to get a job. Until then, he looked after the family.

All four children were christened into the Catholic faith. Keith and Barrie went to a Catholic school, St Joseph's in Derby, but Gail and Cynthia went to the local school at Sinfin. They had a strict upbringing – Keith remembers his father would never tolerate any bad language – but it formed a strong family bond that has helped them through their troubles.

Flo was forty-seven when Gail became pregnant with Lynn. At first she thought she would be too old to cope with a young baby again but she says, 'When Lynn came into the house she melted all our hearts. We decided to keep her, even though she had been half-promised to a couple from Nottingham who wanted to adopt her.'

The pretty little baby fitted smoothly into the family routine. Keith, by then working as an electrician, said he would give his mother a bit of extra money every week to help to pay the additional bills.

Barrie was away in the Far East in the Navy. Curiously, even though he hadn't been told about Gail's pregnancy, he wrote a letter home saying he had dreamed about a baby in the house.

Cynthia, until Lynn arrived, was the youngest and according to her mother an impetuous tomboy, always in trouble at school. But she played her part too in Lynn's upbringing. Cynthia finished work earlier than her mother, and every day she would pick up Lynn at the nursery school and take her home. Her grandmother recalls:

The little girl charmed everybody. We used to dress her up in pretty dresses – she always liked to look nice – and take her with us on a lot of coach trips. She would sing nursery rhymes which she had been taught at school – 'Twinkle Twinkle Little Star', and little songs like that. She would get the whole bus joining in the singing. She grew up in an atmosphere of love, and all the family doted on her.

That is why it was so hard to accept her cruel death. Her killers took away something that was precious to the whole family. That was why we all agreed they must never be allowed to get away with it.

11 'Who Killed Lynn Siddons?'

After the trial, the Brookes family were not at all happy living just a few doors away from the Siddons family. Michael Brookes was shunned by his neighbours and one evening when he went out for a drink, a group of girls spat at him.

Another morning his wife drew the curtains to find somebody had daubed the word 'Murderer' in white paint on the path in front of their house, and hung a rope in the shape of a noose above their door.

Bricks were thrown at the house, and some smashed through the windows. But the incident that made up their minds to move away from Carlyle Street involved Tracey, their daughter, by now seven years old.

Three boys, aged about eleven, put a rope around her neck one day on the recreation ground in Sinfin. According to her father, they tried to strangle her. Luckily, a neighbour saw them and intervened. When Tracey got home she had scorch marks on her neck from the rope.

Her parents decided there and then they would try to find a home elsewhere, and the council offered them a house in another part of the city. But if they hoped to get away from Lynn's avengers and memories of the murdered girl, they were sadly mistaken.

Flo Siddons and her family soon discovered a great well of sympathy over Lynn's death – and anger at the fact that her killers seemed to have escaped retribution. Flo says:

Wherever we went around Sinfin, people would come up to us and say how sorry they were and what a terrible shame it was that her murderers had got away with it. It was the same when we went shopping in Derby.

Our pictures had been in the newspapers and on TV, and we were recognized wherever we went. If we were shopping or whatever we were doing, people would come up, most of them strangers, and say how sorry they were.

With such a network of spies and sympathizers, it wasn't long before somebody whispered the Brookes' new address into Flo's ear – 59 Macklin Street, not far from the city centre.

But before they launched their crusade of deliberate harassment, Flo and her family decided to try to mount a legitimate campaign to bring Lynn's killers to justice.

They were amazed, as were many people throughout the city, that the police had not stepped in immediately after the trial, arrested Michael Brookes, and charged him with the murder.

But as the weeks slipped by and there was no apparent action by the police, the family got more and more fed up, and decided to tackle Phillip Whitehead, the Labour MP for Derby North, about the situation.

Whitehead had helped them before at the time Lynn was missing. He had stung the police into issuing a statement and breaking their week-long silence. Now he acted again.

He wrote a letter to the Chief Constable, Walter Stansfield, telling him, if he didn't already know, about the disquiet in the city that a girl had been brutally stabbed to death and nobody was facing a murder charge.

The police replied there was no evidence against Michael Brookes, so he could not be charged. And even though they claimed the investigation was still alive, the Siddons family saw no signs of anything to convince them that the hunt for Lynn's killers was still being actively pursued.

In the early weeks of 1979, Flo, Gail and Cynthia sat in the lounge at Carlyle Street designing posters with the words: 'Who killed Lynn Siddons?' They were printed in orange ink, and had a photograph of Lynn on them. They invited people who supported the campaign to bring her killers to justice to get in touch with the family.

Other posters had a picture of Michael Brookes on them. Phillip Whitehead gave Flo a friendly hint that she could get into trouble with the law for distributing these, but the family went ahead, plastering the city with them. They were not worried about trouble with the law.

Hundreds of posters were distributed. Some were given to drivers to put in car windows. Others were handed to householders to display in windows or pin on trees in their gardens. They were plastered on billboards, the doors of empty properties, even lamp-posts.

Flo said, 'We put an awful lot up in the Macklin Street area. We'd go out at night putting them up wherever we could. The police often saw us at it, but they didn't do anything. A lot of the young bobbies sympathized with us.

'Often we'd go round the next night and find a lot of the posters had been taken down. At one stage we were suspicious Mick Brookes was following us around taking posters down as we put them up.'

The family also decided to collect signatures on a petition, with the wording, 'We are dissatisfied with the handling of the Lynn Siddons case by Derbyshire Constabulary, and disturbed that at this late point the murderer is still at large. We are therefore seeking assurance that the police are still pursuing inquiries and that the case will be speedily concluded.'

People flocked to sign the petition, and, within a few weeks, they had collected thousands of signatures. The cause the Siddons family were pursuing was winning them new allies every day, and on the morning of Saturday, 24 January, the people of Derby were able to measure the strength of their support.

The Siddons family – Flo, Gail and Cynthia – led a procession through the city centre, with Keith and Barrie and other relatives just behind them. The purpose was to collect more signatures, and show the police they meant business. The marchers made their way through the crowds of people doing their weekend shopping. By the time the procession reached the city police headquarters in Full Street, it had been joined by hundreds of people.

Housewives, schoolchildren, pensioners, workmen – all sorts of people filed up behind the banner-carrying Siddons family. Even a group of bikers who had never heard of Lynn Siddons joined the throng. One of them asked, 'What's it all about?' Somebody quickly told him the story, so he and his leather-clad mates joined the procession.

They stood outside the building waving their banners with the message, 'Who killed Lynn Siddons?' They chanted and shouted. Flo heard later that senior detectives who had been working on the investigation were in the police station that morning. She says, 'None of them dared to show their faces. They were probably too embarrassed. They knew who killed Lynn Siddons, but they weren't doing anything about it.'

It was on 6 March that they handed in their petition with more than 6000 names. They asked Phillip Whitehead to accompany them to Derbyshire County Council headquarters at Matlock. This was where the police committee met, and the family were hoping political pressure from members of the committee might spur the police into action.

Again, the three little women, Flo Gail and Cynthia, who were becoming known as the Three Musketeers, went with Phillip Whitehead to hand in the bulky list of names. They were received by an official. But there was no immediate response.

Flo and her family felt badly let down by the police. The name of the man who they knew was the main architect of Lynn's death was on everybody's lips. He had been interviewed in newspapers, and on television. But he was still free.

Michael Brookes continued to deny he had anything to do with Lynn's death. On 2 February 1979 he was interviewd by a BBC reporter for the programme *Midlands Report*. He looked gaunt and pale as he faced the camera, with Dot by his side, and his rubbery lips pouted over his splaying teeth as he kept shaking his head.

He was asked, 'Were you involved in the attack on Lynn Siddons?'

'No, I was not,' he replied.

'In any way?'

'No.'

Then the question was put, 'Do you think that people still believe despite the verdict at the trial that you were involved?'

Brookes answered, 'Quite a few people, yes. I would definitely say so. Since we left Sinfin, I've not really moved out of my home. I've always stayed in the Derby area.

Friends of my family and even my mother has come down here to visit me and told me she's heard people trying to make an accusation against me.'

No matter how much he denied having anything to do with Lynn's murder, the Siddons family knew he was guilty. They were appalled that he had not been charged. If the police had made a mistake in the beginning by charging the wrong person, surely it could be put right now, they reasoned. Why hadn't they charged Michael Brookes? Was it because such an action would show they had made a mistake in the first place by charging Roy – and would virtually be an admission they had blundered? Or was it simply that they didn't have the evidence?

Whatever the reason, Flo and her family felt the detectives were not doing their jobs properly. So they decided to turn detective themselves to see if they could turn up any new evidence that could be used to build up a case against Michael Brookes.

The first thing they did was to ask a treasure hunting club to take their metal detectors down to the canal where Lynn's body was found. The blade of the knife Roy had broken while pressing it against Lynn's stomach had never been found, and neither had the sheath knife the boy said Michael Brookes had plunged repeatedly into her body.

The club members willingly obliged. Like so many people in Derby, they felt sympathy for the Siddonses, and admiration for the way they were pursuing their campaign. On a wet Sunday morning, they took their metal detectors to the canal and spent hours thoroughly covering the area where the body had been hidden. But they found nothing.

Another piece of police work by Flo Siddons did produce a result. After Mick Brookes and his family left 27 Carlyle Street, Gail approached the new tenant, Mick Hardy Thompson, and introduced herself.

Flo and Gail had nosed around the house while it was empty and found the partly-burned pages of girlie magazines. But they suspected more valuable clues might be buried in the garden, and asked Mick Thompson to keep his eyes open if he did any digging.

A month or so later, he was digging the back garden to make a vegetable plot when the spade clanged against something metallic. He bent down and picked up the object. After brushing the soil off it, he saw it was a knife.

Mick Thompson realized his discovery could be highly significant. It could fill in that all-important gap linking Lynn with her murderer. He tried to get in touch with Flo, but she was away for the day, so he telephoned the police.

It was a Saturday morning, and none of the detectives involved in the case were available. But a uniformed constable cycled out from Pear Tree police station, took the knife, put it in his pocket, and cycled away again.

It seems incomprehensible, but somehow the police managed to lose it. The knife, possibly a murder weapon, was mislaid at the police station and has never turned up.

Incredibly, that act of gross negligence was followed by another. A week or so later in a different part of the garden, Mick Thompson dug up some sodden clothing. It looked like a pair of trousers which had been partly burned, and a shirt. He also found a large canvas shoe.

This time he did get hold of the Siddons family. Cynthia went round to the house and put the clothing in a plastic bag which she then took to the family solicitor. He handed it to the police.

It seems mind-boggling, but the police managed to lose this as well. It would be laughable if it were not so serious, like some far-fetched plot from a crime comedy. But these were real articles in a real-life murder mystery, and had the potential to be important pieces of evidence which may have helped to trap a killer.

Later it was officially admitted in a statement from the Director of Public Prosecutions that both the knife and the clothing were missing.

How a police force could misplace, lose, allow to go missing – choose whichever phrase you like – items which might supply vital clues has never been explained. Nor is it known whether those responsible for such carelessness were traced and punished.

After the second discovery in the garden at number 27 Carlyle Street, a team of police officers went to the house and carefully dug over the entire garden.

This was, perhaps, something that should have been done earlier. According to Roy Brookes' statement, two knives were used to kill Lynn, and all that had been recovered was the handle of one of them. In cases where the weapon used for a murder is missing, police normally go to great lengths to try to find it. The digging up of a suspect's garden is usually routine.

But the garden at number 27 yielded no further clues which might have brought justice a step closer for the anxious Siddons family.

12   The Haunting of Michael Brookes

Shortly before eight o'clock every morning, Flo Siddons hurried from her home in Carlyle Street to catch the Number 88 bus from Sinfin into Derby city centre. She could have caught a later bus and still been at work on time, but she needed an extra fifteen minutes or so for what became a compelling part of her daily routine.

Her job at the Norvic shoe factory in Webster Street took her past the Pennine Hotel at the corner of Macklin Street. This was the street where the Brookes family had been given a new home to get them away from the hostility and harassment they encountered in Sinfin after Lynn's murder.

Punctually at 8.30 every morning from Monday to Friday, Flo took up her position outside the Pennine Hotel. She just stood there looking at the house – number 59 – where Mick Brookes and his family lived in the middle of a terrace of similar houses.

Flo stood there, in rain or sunshine, saying nothing, just staring accusingly at the house. She stayed for between fifteen and twenty minutes. Then she walked along to Webster Street to start her job as a shoe machinist.

Mick Brookes never gave an indication that he knew of these morning visitations from the tiny grandmother fixing his home with her piercing gaze. But she says, 'He knew all right – the whole family knew. Sometimes the curtain would twitch. They knew I was there watching them.

'It was quite deliberate. I was haunting him. I wanted to remind him every morning that I knew what he had done. I wanted him to know that he couldn't get away from it.'

Sometimes she would cross the road to the door and put an envelope through the letter box. These letters, which she signed, accused Michael Brookes of stabbing Lynn to death.

Flo was not the only member of the Siddons family to keep up the determined barrage of harassment. Every Friday evening, between 5.30 and 6.30, Gail Halford and her husband John would go to the same position and keep watch on the Brookes house.

Gail says, 'We never said anything or did anything except stand watching the house. We wanted Mick Brookes to believe we had hired somebody to kill him. The idea was to worry him day and night and make sure his conscience got no rest for what he had done to Lynn.'

Somebody was sending him anonymous letters threatening his life. He received a Valentine's Day card two years running with the message, 'We're going to get you.' Brookes reported this to the police, and two detectives came to see Flo to ask her if she was responsible.

She says, 'I told them I wasn't. The letters I was sending Mick Brookes I was quite prepared to sign.'

Cynthia also took part in the vendetta – a more active part. She says, 'We used to go there late at night and smash his windows. Then we'd drive off at high speed. We used a borrowed car so it couldn't be traced to us if anybody got the number.'

One night her husband, Gordon, went to the door and shouted through the letterbox, 'We're coming to burn you out.'

The upstairs window was flung open, and Brookes leaned out wailing, 'Police, police. Please help me. Somebody wants to murder me.'

The Siddons family were determined to keep up the pressure on the man who had killed Lynn, and his wife Dot who they thought was shielding him. They had more posters printed. They stuck them on lamp-posts all round the Macklin Street area.

Flo says, 'It was a deliberate campaign. We wanted to make life hell for him. We wanted to worry him day and night so that he didn't get a moment's peace. He may have got away with it legally and kept his freedom, but we were making sure he didn't enjoy it.'

Brookes was getting aggravation on another front. His daughter, Tracey, was being taunted by her classmates at school with chants like, 'Your dad's a murderer.'

Just before Christmas that year, Flo saw Mick and Roy Brookes shopping in Woolworths on The Spot near the centre of Derby. She could see Brookes with his six feet height standing above other shoppers but Flo, just five feet tall, was lost in the crowd.

She edged her way nearer and nearer to the man she despised and, when just a few feet away, she hissed in a loud stage whisper, 'Murdering bastard!'

It was not loud enough to cause a scene in the store, but Brookes picked up the words from the tiny ghost who was haunting him. He grabbed Roy's hand and they rushed out into the street and disappeared among the crowds of Christmas shoppers on London Road.

Mick Brookes, by now thirty-five, had had just about enough. He felt himself succumbing to the pressure. It was coming at him like a rugby pack with Flo in the front row, Gail and Cynthia close behind, and their husbands and brothers forming a supportive back-up.

It proved too much, and it swept him away. There was a girl he knew called Carol Dunworth. Carol, a lively young woman of mixed race, was only nineteen, little more than half the age of her unsavoury lover. For some inexplicable reason, she found herself attracted to Brookes and ran off with him. They caught a train to Skegness, and they hoped to get jobs working at a fairground in Mablethorpe.

Dot Brookes was distraught at losing her husband, especially to a younger woman. The explosive mixture of fury and jealousy unleashed a mad desire to hurt Michael – and the way she could hurt him most was to tell the guilty secret he had confided in her.

Dot went to a telephone box one Sunday morning and rang the one member of the Siddons family she had in her notebook. It was Cynthia's number.

Dot said, 'I want you to come and see me. Mick did it – he killed Lynn. I'll tell you all about it. I'm prepared to make and sign a full statement. I'll even go to court and give evidence against the bastard.'

Cynthia was beside herself with excitement. She arranged to go to the house in Macklin Street right away. But first she rushed off to pick up her mother and her sister.

She says, 'We were overjoyed. This was the breakthrough

we had been waiting for. We thought that with a statement from Dot Brookes we could put Mick where he belonged – in the dock.'

The three women presented themselves at the door of 59 Macklin Street, and Dot Brookes invited them in. She told them how she had caught her husband trying to burn his trousers a couple of days after the murder, and she told them he had confessed that he had killed Lynn.

The next morning Florence and Gail went to see their solicitor, John Vinnicombe. He arranged for a retired police superintendent, Ossie Lloyd, who did some work for him, to go and see Dot Brookes and write down her statement.

First she told him about her bizarre sex life with Mick, how he would prod her with his finger, and pretend to stab her with a knife, as a prelude to making love.

She also told about a sheath knife kept on top of a wardrobe in their bedroom at Sinfin. She asked Michael about it and he said he did not know how it got there. She wanted to get rid of it, but he told her to leave it where it was. She said in her statement:

> I did put the sheath knife in the dustbin but it seemed to turn up in the house again. I asked Roy about it because he had told me it was his knife. This was why I threw it away. When I asked Roy about the knife when it turned up again, he said he knew nothing about it.
> I was cleaning Roy's room out and when doing this I found a suede type of sheath and I thought about the sheath knife. I asked Roy if he had the knife and he said he hadn't, so I pointed out the sheath to him and he said that was all he had left now. I saw no harm in him keeping the sheath, and it was left in the bedroom.

The Siddons family believe that this was the sheath knife used to kill Lynn. It has never been found.

Dot then began to talk about some of the girlfriends her husband had been with during their marriage, and how he liked young girls. But she said, 'As far as I know, Michael never tried to do anything to the girls who came to the house to see Roy. Lynn Siddons would ask Roy to walk down to her home with her when it was dark but she would not let Michael walk with her.'

Dot then gave her version of events on the day Lynn had vanished. Lynn had agreed to go with Roy to see about the farm job his stepfather had talked about. First she had gone home to take off her shoes and put on boots for the walk across the fields.

When Roy had returned, he said Lynn had gone off while he went into the trees for a pee. Dot Brookes said in her statement, 'Roy did not seem strange in his manner. One thing which I thought was unusual he did not come in and sit down in the room. He just stood in the doorway. He did not look any different to when he went out. He was not uneasy.'

She said that when Mick got home and she told him about Lynn going off, he had replied, 'Oh, leave her. She will come back when she is ready.'

During the week before Lynn's body was discovered, the police questioned Roy Brookes several times. Dot said, 'Michael seemed to be keeping very close to Roy that week. Roy was staying up late – he was very worried. When I tried to question Roy, Michael used to tell me to leave him alone.'

The next part of Dot's statement gave details about her husband's strange behaviour on the Monday Lynn was murdered, and the days which followed:

I recall that when Michael came home on the Monday afternoon, he had gone into the bathroom as soon as he came into the house. The bathroom is on the ground floor, and he had gone upstairs after and when he came down I saw he had changed his trousers.

Several days later, after the police had been to the house a lot, I came into the living room and I found Michael and he was making a fire and he had the trousers in his hand and he burnt them on the fire.

I asked him why he was doing this, and he said they were torn. I asked him to let me see them and said that if they were torn in the seam I could mend them but he would not let me see them.

I also saw him burn the sheath knife. I asked him why he was doing this and he said he had seen it either in the bathroom or upstairs, but he gave me no reason for burning it.

The next morning Michael cleaned the fireplace out. I saw that he put the ashes in the dustbin.

Dot continued to tell how she had kept on at her husband after Roy's trial to tell her exactly what had happened. Roy had said in his second statement that Michael Brookes was the killer. Was the boy telling the truth, or was it a lie to save his own skin? The words were written down as she uttered them:

I was always on to him as I felt that sooner or later he would tell me what had happened. Every time I spoke to him he was worried. When the Government was discussing the return of capital punishment, Michael was concerned about this and said if they ever found out anything he would get hung.

When I asked him what they could find out, he very angrily said 'Nothing'. I knew he was on edge.

It was about the end of March. Michael and I was in the house together and I was getting on to him to tell me. He was convinced the police had bugged the house.

I was talking about Lynn and how she had been left down in the woods and he turned to me and said, 'You are on about that again.'

I said it must have been terrible what she had gone through down there. He then said, 'If you must know, I did kill Lynn and I fucking enjoyed it.'

Dot's statement then gave the version of Lynn's killing as she had heard it from her husband:

I was flabbergasted, and Michael then told me that they had gone up the street with Lynn and he had gone to Sinfin Lane and had telephoned his mother and found that she was not in. 'This was my alibi.'

He said he had rushed down Sinfin Lane and out across the golf course to cut them off. He was at the edge of the field when he was going down and Lynn had asked him what he was doing there. He said to me that 'she soon knew what I was fucking doing down there'.

Michael said they had all walked along the canal and he was behind Lynn and Roy and they went in these bushes and he came behind Lynn and put his arm right round her neck to hold her and he wanted Roy to hit her or something and he wouldn't do it.

He said 'I told Lynn I had a present for her' and she had asked what it was and he had a knife and stuck it in. He said

Roy would not do anything. 'He's like all the blacks. He is a yellow bastard. He's got no guts. He was all talk and no action.'

I said, 'Why should you do that? She has done you no harm.'

He said, 'She's like the rest of them. She is a slut.'

I asked him, 'What did happen in the woods?'

He said, 'I kept stabbing her but she wouldn't die.'

I asked him what Roy was doing and he said 'He stood trembling and was frightened.'

He went on to say he dragged her to some water and he put her head down in it and he held her down with his hands in it and put his foot on her head, not hard, but enough to keep her head down. He said that when he turned her over he saw soil in her mouth and he said he put a load of soil in her mouth. He said 'Roy would not help me.'

He said he dragged her back and put her where no-one could find her.

When I asked him about the wounds on her, he turned round and said he tried to stab her through her jeans but the knife would not go in at first so he undid her zip and stabbed her that way with the zip open. He said he got his two hands on the knife and tried to rip her down but it was too hard.

I asked him about her clothes and he said he had pulled them up to make it look when she was found if someone had tried to rape her.

I said that Roy had to go through all that because of him. He said, 'If he had kept his mouth shut none of this would have happened. But he couldn't.'

He said he had told Roy what to say. 'I am in all this trouble through him opening his mouth.'

He said, 'I had the laugh of them in court and I have the laugh of them again.'

He said, 'They will never hold me because there will be a number two before they get me. I can only be done for one.'

He also said, 'If you open your mouth to the law, you will end up like Lynn. Because the next time I will make a bloody good job of it.'

It took nearly four hours for Dot Brookes to tell the whole of her story – from 9.30 in the morning until 1.20. The statement is dated 30 April 1980, signed D. M. Brookes, and witnessed by Ossie Lloyd.

She made a similar statement to Phillip Whitehead's

researcher, Helen Goodman, which was handed over to the police. And she asked the Siddons family to do something for her in return. Would they go to Mablethorpe, and find Mick Brookes? Dot couldn't bear the thought of him enjoying himself with another woman, a younger woman. She wanted revenge.

And she asked Flo Siddons to bring her a tape-recorder. 'When Mick comes back, I'll turn it on and put it under the bed,' she promised. 'I'll get him to talk all about the murder and what he did to Lynn while we're making love. You'll have your confession all on the tape.'

The Siddons family were elated. With Dot's confession, the police would have to act and charge Mick Brookes. Flo said to her daughters, 'He'll soon be behind bars where he belongs.'

13   Aunt Cynthia's Revenge

The two cars sped along the A158 on the road from Lincoln to the coast. John Halford was at the wheel of the first car with Gail by his side and his mother-in-law, Flo Siddons, sitting in the back seat with a family friend. Cynthia Smith was driving the second car with her husband Gordon by her side.

It was a bright Sunday morning in May 1980 and the Siddons family were in high spirits. The statement Dot Brookes had made named her husband Michael Brookes as Lynn's killer and armed with this hard evidence they were on their way to confront him.

They knew he had gone to Mablethorpe with his latest girlfriend, Carol Dunworth. They had been told he was planning to get a job at a funfair. They had pictures of Mick Brookes and a good description of Carol, a black girl. The Siddons family were getting used to detective work. Brookes and his girlfriend should not be too difficult to find.

At the fair they split up into two groups so they could get around the stallholders, roundabouts and swings more quickly. There was no sign of Brookes working on any of the rides or sideshows so they began to flash his picture around and quiz the fairground workers.

One or two of them thought the face looked familiar, but they were not sure. Some said he had worked there for a short time but had then moved on. It looked as if their enquiries were going to draw a blank. But then Gail had a stroke of luck.

She went to a group of men who were operating the dodgem track and showed them a poster with Mick's picture on it. One of the men immediately recognized him.

'Yes ... Mick,' he said. 'That was his name. But he moved

on a few days ago.'

Gail looked crestfallen. 'Did he say where he was going?'

The man replied, 'I don't know where he's working ... but I know where he's living. He's rented a caravan just outside Skegness. In somebody's back garden, he told me.'

Gail was so delighted she felt like kissing the helpful worker. 'Thanks,' she said. 'That's great.' And she rushed off to find the rest of the family to tell them what she had discovered.

Soon the convoy was on the move again to Skegness eighteen miles down the coast. They knew it wasn't going to be easy. There would be scores of caravans around the resort. But the Siddons family had faced problems before, and they were determined to carry out a thorough hunt.

They drove along each road out of Skegness for several miles looking into gardens to see if they could spot a caravan. No luck ... turn around ... try again. It was early evening before they found what they were looking for – an old house, in need of painting and repairs, with a caravan parked in the garden behind it.

They parked the cars and walked towards it, still not certain that it was the right caravan. But then Gail said, 'This is it. I know it is.'

'How do you know?' her sister asked her.

'Just look at that washing.'

There was a line stretching from the caravan to a tree in the garden, with grubby shirts and underclothes hanging out to dry.

'That's Dot Brookes' washing. I've seen her washing before. It's still dirty. She's not very good at it.'

This was an unexpected development, and the family returned to the cars for a conference. That washing on the line meant that Dot Brookes was there. She shouldn't have been. The person in the caravan with Brookes should have been his girlfriend, not his wife, if their information was correct.

It was decided that the men should investigate further, so John and Gordon crept down by the side of the house and approached the caravan. Mick Brookes was having his Sunday dinner and was about to put a potato into his mouth when he saw the two faces at the window. He spluttered and

the potato splashed back into the gravy on his plate. Dot
Brookes was with him, and so was their daughter, Tracey.

John shouted, 'Let's burn the caravan down with them
inside it.' The words, he says, were meant as a frightener.
'We might have done it if it had just been Mick and Dot
there. We were furious at the way she had let us down. But
we certainly wouldn't have done anything with a child inside
the caravan.'

It was obvious Brookes was terrified. All he could do was
wail plaintively, 'Leave us alone.'

The two men went and rejoined the rest of the family, and
they all went off to a nearby pub for a drink. It had been a
long hard day, and finding Mick and Dot together again was
a complication they hadn't expected.

Cynthia was livid. 'She's ratted on us,' she fumed. 'She
gave us that confession just to get us to frighten him. Now
they're back together again.'

If they had known Dot's intentions that evening, the
wrath of the Siddons family would have led to violence.
They would have surely descended on that caravan for a
showdown. Dot Brookes had changed her mind about
informing on her husband. She wanted him back, so she
withdrew the statement she had made to the police.

The breakthrough that the Siddonses hoped would result
in Mick Brookes being charged with Lynn's murder fizzled
out. Once Dot withdrew the statement, there was no case.
The law will not compel a wife to give evidence against her
husband.

But even if they had known all of this, there was not much
they could have done that evening. From the pub window,
they saw a patrol car pull up at the house where the caravan
was parked. Mick Brookes had called the police to protect
him from Lynn's avengers.

All the family were angry that Dot Brookes had changed
her mind, but the angriest of all was Cynthia. It was Cynthia
who Dot kept ringing up. During one of those telephone
calls Cynthia remembers saying to Dot, 'Don't you let us
down. If you ever go back on that statement, I'll have you.'

Cynthia's chance came four months later while working
for a firm that supplied car parts. On 3 September she was
driving along the A6 northwards out of Derby when she

happened to see Brookes and Dot. They were standing by the roadside trying to hitch a lift.

Cynthia felt a surge of excitement. All through the summer she and her relatives had kept up their campaign. They kept vigil outside Brookes' house in Macklin Street. But he had hardly stepped outside the door. This was the first time she had seen them.

She had a load of car parts in the rear of her blue Vauxhall Chevette which she had to deliver to the Derbyshire County Council highways depot at Ambergate. She kept driving wondering what to do – then she began to look for a telephone box.

It occurred to her that Mick and Dot might be trying to get away from Derby – to find some new home where they would be free from the unwelcome attentions of Flo and her daughters. They must not be allowed to get away, Cynthia decided. They would not escape if she could do anything about it.

She found a phone box. The only member of the family she knew she could contact, and who might be able to get away and do something, was Gail's husband, John. She dialled the number. Blast ! It was engaged.

Ambergate is about a half-hour drive from Derby, so she decided to press on. As soon as she got to the highways depot, she made for the office, where the staff knew her, and asked to use the telephone.

This time she got through. 'John. I've seen Mick and Dot Brookes. They're hitch-hiking on the Duffield Road. Can you get away and follow them or something?'

It was an inconvenient time, and John couldn't leave the factory where he worked as a grinder.

Cynthia recalls, 'I felt sick. Lynn's murderer was escaping. We might never be able to find him again.'

She started driving back towards Derby and, as she approached Belper, she had a surprise. There on the roadside were the couple she thought she had lost. The Brookes had either got a lift or caught a bus, and had got as far as Belper, eight miles north of Derby. They were standing on the empty pavement across the road from Belper Fire Station.

According to her mother, Cynthia was always an

impetuous girl, and what happened next was certainly an act of extreme impetuosity. She spun the steering wheel around so that her car slewed across the road and hurtled directly at the Brookes.

The pair of them ran across the road to get out of the way of the careering vehicle. But Cynthia hadn't finished. She spun the car round and chased them into the lay-by outside the fire station. Mick Brookes had to put his hand on the bonnet and vault over a low wall to escape.

The pair of them climbed a low embankment so that Cynthia could not pursue them. She sat there with the engine of her car still running, daring them to come down. But they didn't.

Mick Brookes went down the other side of the embankment and tried to flag down a couple of cars, but nobody stopped, so the pair of them ran to the convent just along the road and sought sanctuary with the nuns.

Looking back on the incident, Cynthia says:

> I don't know what was in my mind. I don't think I intended to run them over. I hate Mick Brookes for what happened to Lynn. Every time I see him I think of all the things he did and it churns up my stomach. And I was furious with Dot for going back on her statement.
>
> I don't think I have it in me to kill. But I just didn't want them to get away. I just took my car across the road and drove it at them, going right up on to the kerb.
>
> The A6 is a busy road, but luckily nothing was coming so I was able to drive across the road. I wasn't in a blind red rage as I remember checking in my mirror that there was nothing coming before chasing them over to the other side of the road.
>
> I think my intention was to frighten them, to give them a really good scare. They wondered what I was going to do when they were on the embankment. They were only ten yards away from me. It was real eyeball-to-eyeball stuff before they ran off to the convent.

By this time, the duty fireman had arrived on the scene, wandering what all the commotion was about. Cynthia asked if she could use the telephone. She was crying and upset. She rang Gail, and the fireman overheard her saying, 'If he comes out, I'll kill him. I hate him.'

She admits she was in a state of near hysteria, but it passed over and soon she was back to normal. In fact, that evening she went to see Derby County playing a football match. But she had a surprise on the way home when she called for a drink at her local pub, The Victoria, which also happened to be the local for one of the detectives who had been investigating Lynn's murder.

Cynthia knew and liked Inspector Arthur Padmore. But that evening his opening remark came as a shock to her.

'Who's been a naughty girl?'

She thought he was joking. 'You tell me.'

Padmore said, 'You know what I'm talking about.'

'No I don't,' Cynthia said.

'You tried to run Mick Brookes down,' the inspector said.

'Oh, come off it,' Cynthia said flippantly.

When Brookes and his wife had run into the convent, they had telephoned the police. He had said Cynthia deliberately tried to run the pair of them down. But Cynthia didn't take the accusation seriously. In her mind, the whole incident had been a frightener, not a serious attempt to injure them.

Nothing else was said that night in The Victoria, but the following morning Cynthia was to discover her little indiscretion was being taken seriously, very seriously. It was the friendly Inspector Padmore who told her on the telephone she'd better get along to Alfreton police station where the incident was being dealt with

'I can't go now,' she said. 'I'm busy.'

Inspector Padmore replied grimly, 'You'd better go – or they'll come and fetch you.'

At Alfreton, she found herself facing a barrage of searching questions. Then the police took her spectacles, jewellery and tights from her and locked her in a cell.

As the time drifted by, she began to realize she was in big trouble. She started crying and beating the door with her hands. The cries gave way to screams. Soon she was hysterical.

She recalls, 'I'd never been in trouble before, and here I was in a cell. I kept thinking about my kids – they were in school and there would be nobody to meet them. I don't think I've ever been so upset.'

Then a pair of CID officers came to the cell, and began to

question her all over again.

'I want you to tell me what you did.'

'I've told you,' she sobbed.

'You tried to kill Brookes, didn't you?'

'No I didn't.'

Eventually she said, 'Just write it down and give me the paper and I'll sign it. I'll sign anything to get away from here.'

But the policemen shook their heads and one of them said, 'Oh, no. We can't do that. Your family's been shooting their mouths off about how the police don't do their job. If I don't have you before the court in the morning, I'm not doing my job, am I?'

Soon afterwards Gail and her husband John arrived. By that time Cynthia had been in police custody for three hours. They arranged bail. After more formalities, Cynthia was allowed to leave.

But even though she was free once more, she took with her a terrible worry. The charge on the bail forms was attempted murder.

The case did not come to court until 30 March 1981, more than seven months after the incident. It was adjourned no less than four times because of the non-appearance of the vital witnesses, Mick Brookes and his wife. They were in no hurry to face the Siddons family, it seems, even in the secure environment of a police court.

The hearing was at Alfreton. In the interval, the charge had been reduced. Cynthia Smith was no longer being accused of attempted murder, but reckless driving, to which she pleaded not guilty.

This meant that Dot Brookes would have to go in the witness box, which is precisely what the Siddonses wanted. That way their solicitor, Bernard Hawcroft, could cross-examine her, and try to wrest the truth for the real motive behind Cynthia's action.

Mr Hawcroft asked Dot about the telephone call she made to Cynthia at the time her husband was living apart from her, in which she said he had confessed to Lynn's murder, thereby confirming her statement to the police.

Hawcroft: 'You said your husband admitted being respon-

sible for the murder of Lynn Siddons?'
Dot Brookes: 'Yes I did.'
Hawcroft: 'Do you believe it had any foundation?'
Dot Brookes: 'I refuse to answer that question.'
Hawcroft: 'Why?'
Dot Brookes: 'Because it's got nothing to do with this.'
Hawcroft: 'It was a serious allegation to make.'
Dot Brookes: 'It's nothing to do with this case or with anyone else.'

Dot Brookes was quite adamant. She refused to give any explanation why she had made the statement, and then retracted it, to the police and the Siddons family lawyers

Cynthia was found guilty of the reckless driving charge and fined £100. Altogether, with costs and legal fees, the bill for her moment of madness came to more than £400.

But the case had an important side effect which proved to be crucial in the campaign. Because Brookes' name had been mentioned in court, it enabled newspapers to report on the background without fear of libel or contempt proceedings.

While the case was being heard at Alfreton, Flo Siddons sat silently clutching her handbag. From time to time, she would throw a hate-filled glance at the man who was being named as Lynn's murderer.

It was as well there was a distance of several feet between them. Flo now admits that in her bag that day she had a bottle of acid and, given a chance, she would have hurled it into the leering face of her sworn enemy.

14 Inside Information

The reckless driving case against Cynthia Smith made headlines in most of the newspapers – 'The Vengeance of Auntie Cynthia' screamed the *Sun*. It highlighted the Siddons family's crusade for justice. But what it didn't do was to produce fresh evidence that would bring Michael Brookes to trial.

If the police were still investigating Lynn's murder, there were no signs of it. So the family held a conference at the house in Carlyle Street to decide what to do next.

By now Mick Brookes and his family had moved yet again to try to get away from the harassment and those early morning spectral visitations by Flo Siddons. They had been allocated a house in Beaufort Street, again not far from the centre of Derby.

It was not long before the Siddons, through their network of contacts, picked up the new address. They were, by now, beginning to realise that although worrying and tormenting Lynn's killers gave them a sense of relief, it was not achieving their main aim – to bring them to justice.

At the conference, Keith, Flo's eldest son, who works as an electrician, favoured a different approach. Although he supported the family Keith had not taken an active part in those raids on the Brookes' house. He thought the campaign should vary its direction slightly.

'Somebody must know something,' he said. 'Why don't we get an appeal published in the newspapers? It might turn up something new.'

The appeal duly appeared as a story in the *Derby Trader* and something new did turn up. That crumpled copy of the *Trader* found its way into Leicester Prison and was passed around the inmates. It was read by a burglar called Keith

Hibbert who showed it to his cellmate Clive Shirtcliffe.

Hibbert and Shirtcliffe had a long history of petty crime. But, like many old lags, they had a code of honour. And the murder of a young girl had no place in that code.

Hibbert reminded Shirtcliffe of a drinking session they had been involved in years before when they had finished up at a bar called Jimmy's.

Holding the newspaper, he said, 'This is what it's all about. Remember that bloke who came up to me? That was Mick Brookes. He said he was involved in this girl's murder.'

Because of family complications, Hibbert was loath to tell the police. But Shirtcliffe decided something had to be done. He wrote a letter and sent it to Phillip Whitehead, the MP who had been campaigning on behalf of the Siddons family and whose name was mentioned in the article.

The police eventually came to see Keith Hibbert and the full story emerged. He had known Mick Brookes as a lad. The pair of them had been in trouble with the law. Hibbert later repeated his statement to a solicitor acting for the Siddons family:

> I attended Derby Magistrates Court on a date I cannot now remember and successfully applied for bail. Roy Brookes was also present – his appearance was just before mine. I noticed Mick Brookes in court.
>
> After I was released I went for a drink with Clive Shirtcliffe, Douggie Smith and several others. We went to a number of different pubs. I noticed Mick in the first pub and then the second and then in Jimmy's (St James Hotel).
>
> In Jimmy's I was standing near the bar with the others and Mick was standing behind me. I can't remember who spoke to who first. He asked me if he could have a word with me. We went and sat down. I can't remember the exact words of the conversation but it was about the murder of Lynn Siddons. I had not heard of this.
>
> He asked me if I had seen 'his lad'. He explained that he had been up for that murder and I realised the one he was talking about. As that lad was black, I said something like 'What's it to do with you?' and he said he was his lad.
>
> Mick asked how to get a message to him. I replied something to the effect that I couldn't help. Mick seemed to know that if you were done for something like child murder

or rape you had to go on rule 43. He asked me what it was like. I said nobody wants to know you.

At some point I asked him why he was asking these questions. He told me he was involved as well as Roy. The impression I got was that they had both murdered her. I cannot remember what words he used. When I realised, I walked off.

In his statement Hibbert said, 'Shirty kept telling me I ought to tell the police because it was such a horrible thing that Mick had done. I told him I didn't want to because my sister Carol was married to Mick's brother, Bernard, and their marriage was going through difficulties.'

For a while he was not prepared to talk to the police, or agree to give a statement, because he did not want to involve his sister and her marriage difficulties. But later he spoke to his sister and she told him not to worry about her.

Hibbert knew Brookes when he was a young teenager. He used to visit him at his home in Stanhope Street. Even then, Mick liked playing with knives.

Hibbert said, 'I went round to Mick's home. He had a carving knife. He pulled his cardigan up and put the tip of the knife near his belly button. I remember he was holding it with both hands and said to me, "Go on – push it in".'

He recalled another curious incident while the pair of them were on holiday in Skegness. They were playing barefoot on the beach, and Mick trod on a sliver of glass.

Hibbert said, 'It was bleeding very heavily. He just sat there squeezing it and pulling at it. There was quite a lot of blood. He was in no hurry to get back to have it looked at.'

Keith Hibbert also witnessed Mick Brookes' habit of throwing darts at pictures of nude women. He visited Brookes when he came out of approved school and said, 'He had a dartboard in his bedroom. He had posters of nude women on it. He used to throw darts at the pictures of the women. As far as I remember, if he hit a breast he would say something like "Got her".'

The statements which Hibbert and Shirtcliffe made to the police were checked out and sent to the Director of Public Prosecutions. But he decided, probably because of the criminal records of both men, that the statements were not strong enough to warrant a charge being made against Michael Brookes.

In April 1981, however, a new chief constable was appointed for Derbyshire, Alfred Parrish. Flo arranged to meet him. Alf Parrish was disturbed about some aspects of the way his force had handled the murder case, and he ordered a fresh investigation.

Chief Superintendent Jim Reddington and Superintendent Roy Morton, two highly experienced detectives, were in charge. They arranged for all the witnesses to be re-interviewed and themselves went through the mass of evidence with a fine toothcomb.

That investigation lasted almost a year, and produced some new evidence. The two police officers set off with their files to see the Director of Public Prosecutions. But once again the DPP decided there was insufficient admissible evidence to mount a successful prosecution against Michael Brookes.

After more than three years' plotting and planning, campaigning and playing private detectives, the decision came as a severe blow to Flo. It was the first of many such knock-backs, but she and her family with their enormous resilience have always come up fighting.

They got in touch with Phillip Whitehead, the MP who had been so helpful at the time of Lynn's disappearance. They had been to see him at his Friday night surgery in North Derby so often they had become friendly with him, and he agreed to take up their case with the Director of Public Prosecutions.

Phillip Whitehead wrote a long letter to the Attorney General, Sir Michael Havers, setting out the reasons why Michael Brookes should be tried for Lynn's murder.

He argued that if no-one was charged with the murder, it would remain a blot on the record of the Derbyshire police, and a threat to all other women in the city. If he was found guilty, a murderer would have been convicted. If he was found not guilty, then at least his name would be cleared.

And Mr Whitehead made an important final point. If Michael Brookes was not even brought to trial, the police would never be able to counter the charge that they were trying to cover up their initial mistake of charging Roy Brookes on the basis of his dubious first confession.

In October 1982, Sir Michael replied that he would look

closely into every aspect of the case. But three months later, after a long hard look at the file, he announced that he would not sanction a prosecution.

But Phillip Whitehead was still not finished. He raised the subject in Parliament on 18 April 1983. He asked the Attorney General what considerations had led him to decide that a prosecution for the murder of Lynn Siddons at Derby could not presently be brought and what steps he planned to continue consideration of the case.

The Attorney General replied, 'The Decision of the Director of Public Prosecutions was based solely on the insufficiency of the evidence. I personally have considered the papers and I am satisfied it was the correct decision.'

But he went on, 'There is no time limit on the institution of proceedings for murder and the matter can be revived at any time if fresh evidence emerges.'

The Hansard record of this exchange shows that Phillip Whitehead then asked:

I am grateful to the Attorney General for his personal consideration of this matter. Is he aware of the grave disquiet in Derby that no one has been brought to book for this appalling crime after one unsuccessful prosecution? While no one wishes to prejudice the fair trial of any named individual, police investigations must continue until evidence is complete to justify a prosecution.

Sir Michael replied:

I shall limit myself to saying the existing position is one of evidential difficulties. If any further evidence emerges, the matter will be reviewed immediately. The book is not shut. The entire issue will remain open. I hope that some evidence will come forward in the near future to enable this unsatisfactory state of affairs to be resolved.

This put the ball back at the feet of Derbyshire police force. The Siddonses had done their bit to gather evidence, but it seemed to have been rejected.

There are strict rules governing the admissibility of evidence in trials. One of the Siddonses' greatest triumphs was wresting a statement from Dot Brookes maintaining her husband had confessed to Lynn's murder. She had later withdrawn it, but the Siddonses had a signed and witnessed copy of the statement.

This, unfortunately for the Siddons family, would not have been admissible, as Dot Brookes would not have gone to court willingly, and Halsbury's *Laws of England* states unequivocally that witnesses cannot be compelled to testify against their spouses.

But even if they could not get the fresh evidence vital to charge the killer, the police were active on another front. They knew that sympathy was growing every day for the Siddonses, and more people were joining their campaign.

Michael Brookes' picture had appeared on posters, in newspapers and on television. Hundreds of people in Derby knew that face well with its sallow complexion, and thick lips. He was likely to be recognized wherever he went – and that could be a source of trouble if he was attacked.

The police and social workers got together for a case conference to find a way of avoiding this trouble – and moves began to get Brookes out of the city to start a new life elsewhere.

It was about this time that Brookes gave an interview, his last, to the *Derby Trader* which reported how he and his family had suffered three years of abuse, assault and harassment from the Siddonses to get the case reopened. Mick Brookes said:

> I didn't kill Lynn and I will not admit to something I didn't do just to stop this campaign. My life has been made hell these last three years and even if I was charged with the murder I would never get a fair trial.
>
> I have been barred from nightclubs, had bricks thrown through my window and insults hurled at me and my family as we walk around the city.
>
> I never go out now. I'm a prisoner in my own house. Last time I went into a pub I was spat on by a group of girls.

The reporter from the *Trader* asked him what of the statement Dot made and later retracted – that he had admitted murdering Lynn.

He replied, 'A lot of people think I came back to Dot because of that statement to make her take it back. That wasn't it. I came back to see Tracey because she wouldn't let Tracey come and see me.'

He was also asked about the statement Keith Hibbert made. Brookes said, 'That's a bare-faced lie. I remember seeing him in a pub at the time he says but I never said what he reckons I said. I want him to come forward and prove it. Why hasn't he brought it up before.'

Mick Brookes revealed in this interview that he had been questioned in connection with two other local crimes, one a murder, but subsequently released.

He also said he had been interviewed by detectives from Leeds who were hunting for the Yorkshire Ripper, the name given to the serial killer who had hacked to death twelve women, most of them prostitutes, in Yorkshire and Lancashire; Peter Sutcliffe was arrested and convicted in 1983 of these murders.

Brookes added, 'I really dread picking up the paper and reading about a murder or assault. I know I will be suspected not only by the police but by everyone who recognises me.'

Finally he was asked how he felt about the suffering of the Siddons family since Lynn's death.

He said, 'I am sympathetic, of course, but what can I do to satisfy them? I am not going to admit to something I didn't do.'

15   Brookes the Braggart

Mick Brookes boasted that he had murdered Lynn Siddons to at least five people. In a fit of temper, he told his wife Dot. While lovemaking in the caravan at Skegness, he told his mistress Carol Dunworth. He confided in an ex-prisoner, Keith Hibbert, whom he met in a pub. He joked about the killing to a neighbour. And he confessed it to a man with whom he exchanged houses within a couple of hours of meeting him.

When he moved to 44 Beaufort Street in a vain attempt to escape from the avenging Siddons family, he changed his name to Goodwood. But he made no real effort to conceal his identity, and people in the close and friendly neighbourhood around his new home soon came to realize who he was.

It was not long before the Siddons family were given the new address. They knew their network of contacts would keep them informed and make sure that, wherever he went, there would be no hiding place for Mick Brookes.

His evil reputation had spread throughout Derby, and the people of Beaufort Street were horrified when they discovered they had, in their midst, a man and a youth who had brutally killed a young girl.

He became known as Murderer Mick, or Mick the Murderer and he seemed to enjoy his notoriety. At night he loped around the streets wearing an ankle-length dark blue flasher raincoat, cutting a sinister figure in the eerie yellow glare of the sodium lights.

His next-door neighbours in Beaufort Street were George and Maureen Bailey. Their daughter Leander, then sixteen, became one of the succession of teenage girls who were sucked into the weird social life of the Brookes'.

One evening Leander went with Mick, Dot, Roy and Tracey to a funfair in Derby. When she was not home by 9.30 pm, her mother became frantic. She went out into the streets to look for Leander, and met the group walking back home.

Maureen Bailey recalls, 'I was mad. I launched into Mick Brookes. I told him I didn't want my daughter finishing up like Lynn Siddons.'

Brookes replied, 'You've got nothing to fear. I'm not going to hurt her.'

Still furious, Maureen said, 'You'd better not. You touch one hair of her head and I'll kill you myself.'

Beaufort Street is on a council estate off the Nottingham Road, a few minutes' walk from Derby city centre. It had the reputation of being a happy community with a good neighbourly spirit. Children used to play outside the houses and parents knew they would be perfectly safe.

But when the Brookes family came to live amongst them, there was a mounting apprehension. People did not feel so carefree. Mothers told their youngsters to stay in the gardens.

Maureen Bailey says, 'Everybody knew he'd murdered Lynn. People were worried he might try it again. People were afraid while he lived here. We just didn't feel safe with a killer in our midst.'

Maureen warned Leander about going to the house next door, and eventually put a stop to her visits. One afternoon soon afterwards, she bumped into Mick Brookes in the street.

Brookes said to her, 'You think you're big. Can you stand there and tell me you think I killed Lynn Siddons?'

'I told him, "Yes, you did",' says Maureen.

Brookes stood in front of her, his lips curled back in a smug leer. 'Ah, but I'm clever,' he said. 'I'm very clever. You've got to have a damned good memory to be clever, and you've got to be clever to be a good liar. I'm a damned good liar.'

While she was visiting the Brookes' house, Leander, now married and called Bradshaw, recalls that Dot often fished into her large imitation leather black bag and took out a dark blue diary. Leander says:

I got on well with Dot. She used to read parts of the diary to me. She read me parts where Lynn used to come to their house and play cards, and she told me all about Mick running away with his coloured girlfriend and living in a caravan.

But there was one part, for the April of 1978, which she never read to me. That was when Lynn was killed. She showed me where she had written in the pages for those dates, but she wouldn't let me read it.

I asked her why not. She clutched the diary, held it to her breast and said, 'This is the key – Mick will never leave me while I've got this. This is my security.'

Maureen was speaking to Dot one day. She says, 'I just asked her straight out, "Do you think Mick murdered Lynn?" She said she was sure he had.'

One evening Maureen and her family and other neighbours were all invited round to the Brookes' for a get-together. Dot appeared in a black and white rock 'n' roll dress, fitting at the waist and with a flared out skirt with lots of underskirts.

She told the group the pretty dress had belonged to Lynn Siddons. Lynn had loaned it to her while she was still alive – and now that Lynn was dead it was her favourite dress.

At this party Maureen asked Dot, 'Aren't you scared of sleeping with Mick ?'

Dot replied, 'No, I'm the safest thing to him – and he knows it.'

'What do you mean by that ?' Maureen asked.

'My little book tells a lot,' Dot smiled.

She told Maureen about his habit of pretending to stab her with his fingers while she was lying naked or nearly naked across the bed with her head hanging over the edge.

According to Maureen she said, 'He is sick. He does this instead of having proper sex. It does scare me a little bit sometimes.'

But the social occasions became fewer as more people came to know that Mr Goodwood was really Mick Brookes. Neighbours stopped going round. The family became outcasts.

Mick Brookes would sit at home playing his train record at full volume – an LP with all sorts of train noises on it.

Maureen Bailey said, 'He was a freak with that record. It

was like being on a busy station. One day it was blaring away with all these noises coming out of the window. I asked him why he liked it so much.'

Brookes grinned, 'Me and trains have got a lot in common.'

Maureen said, 'You're sick. Did you murder Lynn to the noises of a train ?'

Brookes kept leering as he went to the cutlery drawer and took out the handle of a carving knife. 'There's the handle. Find the blade,' he said.

'Oh you're sick. You're really sick,' Maureen said.

'You can say what you like but you can't prove anything,' Brookes said. He touched his finger to the side of his head. 'Too clever. I'm too clever.'

Another neighbour who was for a time friendly towards the Brookes when they moved to Beaufort Street was Laurence Winton and his wife Eileen who lived just across the road at number 61. Laurence had a pool table in his house, and Brookes often came in to play.

One evening Gordon, the Winton's 12-year-old son, went over to play with Roy who Dot used to call 'My little chocolate soldier'.

Laurence Winton says, 'Gordon came home and told me he had gone upstairs with Roy to Mick's bedroom, and had seen him throwing a knife at pictures of naked women. I stopped him going to the Brookes', and I stopped inviting Mick here to play pool.'

More and more Mick Brookes became a loner as he wandered the streets in that weird long coat buttoned up to the collar. Leander recalls, 'He looked really spooky. People were frightened of him. Everybody knew he had done the murder, and he seemed quite brazen about it.'

Maureen Bailey told the police about Brookes' boasting, and the diary which they all knew Dot Brookes kept. Did it contain vital evidence which, at a trial, might get the conviction for murder the Siddons family so badly wanted – and put Michael Brookes in prison where they wanted him ?

One of the detectives who had been involved in the investigation into Lynn's murder, Chief Inspector Roy Morton, came to visit the Baileys, but they do not know if a search was made for the diary, or, indeed, if the police pursued any of the information and suspicions they had passed on.

After living in Beaufort Street for almost eighteen months, the Brookes' began to feel the effects of the hostility of their neighbours. One night stones came crashing through their windows, and Roy, a pupil at Derby Technical College, suffered as well. Some of his classmates painted graffiti on a wall saying he was a murderer.

Mick Brookes began to realize he and his family were being ostracized in the once friendly street. It was time to move again. He knew that wherever he went in Derby, the Siddons family would soon find out where he was hiding, and continue their vendetta.

So he decided he would move to a different town and through the police and social workers, an arrangement was made for him to exchange houses with a family who lived in Peterborough.

Shane Morley wanted to return to Derby with his wife and children. That was where his mother lived. He had heard a little about the Lynn Siddons case, but he had no idea at first that the tall man talking to him about the house exchange had been implicated in her murder.

Brookes took his family to the Westwood Estate in Peterborough to see the house where he hoped he could live in privacy away from the avenging Siddonses. While Shane's wife, Lorraine, showed Dot around the house, Shane and Mick sat on a settee watching the children's TV programme, *Tizwazz*.

Shane said, 'Almost right away I realised there was something odd about him. We hardly knew each other – yet he was telling me how much he fancied the pretty programme presenter, Sally James, and how he'd like to give her one.'

Mick Brookes went to the lavatory, leaving Roy with Shane. Shane said to Roy, 'Did you have anything to do with the Lynn Siddons murder?'

Roy, says Shane, replied, 'Yes. My dad did it. But don't say anything.'

Shortly afterwards the two men decided to go off for a drink to the Lord Westwood at the corner of the road. They each had a couple of pints of beer. Mick, said Morley, was affable and chatty, and the subject of Lynn's murder came up.

Shane asked, 'Did you kill Lynn Siddons ?'

Brookes replied, 'Yes.'

At the time Shane Morley did nothing at all about it. He thought it was an idle boast. Brookes was chatting a lot, but Morley did not take it seriously.

It was not until nine years later, when he heard that the Siddons family had won the right to start legal action against Mick and Roy Brookes, that he realized those words Mick Brookes had said could be of significance.

Shane Morley repeated those words under oath in the High Court in London. 'I asked Mick Brookes if he actually killed or murdered Lynn Siddons. He said, "Yes, I did. But they will never catch me".'

His tongue loosened by drink, the arrogant braggart could not resist boasting once again how he had killed Lynn – and how clever he was to get away with it.

16   MP Turns Detective

The telephone rang late on a Friday evening at Mill House in the Derbyshire village of Rowsley. Phillip Whitehead was tired after a hard week at the House of Commons, and looking forward to a relaxed weekend at his country home. When he picked up the receiver, he expected it would be a call from one of his constituents with a problem about housing, or taxes, or employment. But when the caller announced his name, Whitehead felt a surge of excitement.

'I'm Bob Brookes. I understand you've been trying to get in touch with me.'

As Labour MP for Derby North, Phillip Whitehead had become one of the Siddons family's staunchest allies in their long crusade for justice. He had asked questions in parliament, written to law officers, badgered the police. But that Friday night telephone call was to launch him in a new role.

'I certainly have,' he answered, trying to keep his voice calm and reassuring. 'I want to meet you to talk about the Lynn Siddons murder.'

Nearly three years had elapsed since the killing. There was a wider reason, as well as sympathy for Lynn's family, for Whitehead's concern. A young girl had been murdered, and many people suspected they knew the murderer's identity. Yet Michael Brookes was wandering freely about the city and the police seemed powerless to arrest him.

The law, it seemed to the MP, was being turned into a farce. He had studied every detail of the case, and pondered long and hard on the difficulties. The police investigation appeared to have reached a form of stalemate where no progress could be made without fresh evidence. Where could that evidence come from? Who could supply it?

Phillip Whitehead believed that the way forward lay in the past. When a murderer has done his foul deed, he must go somewhere to clean himself up, remove the blood from his clothes and destroy the clues that would link him with the crime. Whitehead was convinced the answer to the dilemma was in 27 Carlyle Street, Sinfin – the home of Michael Brookes.

If only he could build up a picture of exactly what happened in that squalid house on the night of Lynn's killing, and during the days which followed, something might emerge to pin the crime on its vile perpetrator, he reasoned.

Several times he had spoken to senior police officers on the case, including the man in charge, Chief Superintendent Jim Reddington. He wanted them to interview everybody who had been to the house. But the prevailing police view was that if these people had not witnessed the actual killing, their evidence would be hearsay and of no value in securing a conviction.

Frustrated by the lack of action, Whitehead decided to turn detective himself. Who knows? he might be able to dig something up, or find a clue the police had missed. It would not be the first time the amateur sleuth had scored over the professionals.

He knew all about the statement Dot Brookes had made in her fury when Michael had run off with his young lover. His researcher, Helen Goodman, had been with Ossie Lloyd, the retired police officer, who had painstakingly written down her words. But Whitehead also knew Dot's statement could not be used in evidence against her husband.

However, Dot had pointed to another clue. On the night Roy Brookes was arrested, Dot Brookes was demented. She had rung Michael's brother, Bob, and he had gone to 27 Carlyle Street with his girlfriend, Ena.

Phillip Whitehead decided to trace Bob Brookes to see if he could piece together what had happened that fateful night. But he had no idea how to contact him. He had no phone number, no address, and though he had heard Bob

Brookes was a travelling salesman, he didn't even know the name of his employer.

All he could do was put out feelers. He knew members of the Brookes family, including Michael's mother. He had known her before Lynn's murder after trying to help the family when Mrs Brookes' first husband had been made redundant by the Rolls Royce bankruptcy. And he knew them as respectable people outraged by what Michael had done.

Whitehead let it be known on the family grapevine that he wanted to meet Bob Brookes. The response to his feelers was not instant. He had to wait several weeks for the message to filter through. When his telephone rang that Friday night, he had to suppress his elation.

Bob Brookes was extremely cagey. 'I don't really want to get involved,' he said. 'I've tried to tell the police what I know but they just weren't interested.'

'Would you tell me what you wanted to tell them?' asked Whitehead.

'I don't know very much. I don't even know if it would help.'

Phillip Whitehead explained that he was trying to weave together all the threads of incidents and conversation, no matter how trifling they might appear, to build up his picture of what had happened in the Brookes household in Carlyle Street.

He said, 'If we can get that picture, we might get a new lead that will remove the excuse for the police not doing anything.'

Bob Brookes was adamant. 'I'm not making a statement to the police. I've told you, they just weren't interested when I went to them two years ago.'

Again Whitehead had to soothe him. 'I don't want you to tell the police. I want you to tell me.'

There was a long pause. 'I don't really want to be seen around Derby after all this business,' said Brookes.

'I can understand that,' Whitehead said. 'Can I come to your home?'

Again Brookes hesitated. 'I don't want to give you my address. I want to stay out of it.'

'That's all right,' replied Whitehead. 'Can we arrange to

meet somewhere, anywhere? I'll come wherever and whenever you like.'

The unlikely rendezvous they chose had shades of Raymond Chandler about it – a billiard hall on the road between Long Eaton and Brookes' Nottingham home. He said there was a room above the tables where they could have a private chat, and they arranged to meet on the following Sunday just before lunchtime.

Whitehead knew Bob Brookes had a low opinion of his brother. There were three boys in the family – Bernard, Bob and Michael. The others were leading decent, respectable lives. But Michael was the black sheep. Even his looks were different from his brothers. The ugliness of his features seemed to mirror a perverse mind.

Bob had seen Michael getting off a train at Derby station after he had run away with Carol Dunworth. There was no sign of Carol. The first thought that sprung into Bob's mind was that his brother had murdered her, too. He told Dot, 'We thought Mick had bumped Carol off and come back alone.'

There was another remark Bob had made earlier which Phillip Whitehead reflected on as he waited to keep his strange appointment. When the police came to Macklin Street to interview Dot Brookes about her statement to the Siddons family, Bob was present. According to Dot he said:

I have had nothing but trouble from my brother for the last twenty years. My brother is mental and a born liar. He is with a girl (Carol Dunworth) who he has threatened and we are frightened for that girl's safety. The only thing that can help him now is to lock him up in a mental home before he does anyone else harm.

On the Sunday morning, Phillip Whitehead set off in his black Ford Escort on the 30-mile drive to Long Eaton. He soon found the billiard hall, and Bob Brookes, who had been playing snooker, put down his cue and walked over to the MP.

'Where can we talk?' asked Whitehead.

'There's a room upstairs,' Brookes replied.

At first, Brookes was guarded. Whitehead recalls:

The impression I got was of a thoroughly decent man who, like the rest of the family, was appalled by what Michael had done. But there was a loyalty there – in times of trouble you stand by your own. That was why he had rushed round to try to help on the night Fitzroy and Michael were taken off by the police. He told me what had happened when he got there. There was absolute blind panic in the Brookes household.

Bob Brookes would only talk if Phillip Whitehead guaranteed him confidentiality. Whitehead has never revealed details of the conversation, and still regards himself bound by the pledge he gave. But he did say that Ena, Bob's girlfriend, was with him, and the statement she gave much later was similar to Bob's description of what went on in the house.

Ena, an attractive divorcee, lives in Melbourne. She has always asked for her full name and address not to be divulged. This is the statement she gave to a solicitor acting for the Siddons family:

In 1978 Bob Brookes was living with me at Burton-on-Trent. He was unemployed. Sometime in April he received a phone call after which he said, 'They've arrested our Michael. Let's get over there.' He said the arrest was for murder.

We picked up Mr and Mrs Paddy [Bob's mother and stepfather] from their home in St Thomas Road. We went to the Brookes house. Dot let us in. Her mother was already there in the lounge.

Dot ranted on. She talked so much she hardly stopped for breath. We were there in all I would say half-an-hour.

Shortly after we arrived she pointed out marks on the wallpaper on the chimney breast. I saw the cut marks. They were slits. The wallpaper was patterned and very dirty so it wasn't possible to see how many slits there were.

Dot told us there had been posters there. The police had taken them away recently. The pictures were of girls. She told us the slits were caused by the knives Michael used to throw at them.

She said Michael slept with a knife under his pillow and that she had to have sex with a knife at her neck.

I remember clearly her saying, 'Nobody knows what I go through'.

She said, 'The bloody *****'. She then said a swear word

that might have been swine. 'I'll never forgive him for involving our Roy.'

She made it clear to me that she believed Michael had murdered Lynn Siddons, so I asked, 'Wasn't there any blood?'

She said, 'Yes. On Mick's trousers. But we have burnt those.'

She was crying and hysterical. We then left and went back to Mr and Mrs Paddy's home. We finally went home.

Back in the room above the billiard hall, Phillip Whitehead listened as Bob Brookes described, in words very similar to those of his girlfriend, what had happened that dreadful night. It emerged that Bob Brookes had tried to tell his story to the police not once but three times before giving up in disgust.

He said to Whitehead, 'I am not going to volunteer to go to the police again. They knew where I was in 1978 and 1979 and they did bugger all about it.'

After the clandestine meeting ended, Phillip Whitehead drove home thinking about what he had heard. If only the police had listened to Bob Brookes, it could have thrown an entirely new slant on the case. They had charged Fitzroy with Lynn's murder without knowing that his stepfather was a pervert whose hobby was stabbing pictures of women. Also, if the detectives had known that Michael Brookes had burned his bloodstained trousers on the day of the murder, he would have had some serious explaining to do.

Whitehead decided that he would go to the police and tell them what he had learned. He told them that he had spoken to Bob Brookes in confidence, and he had information of material value about the behaviour of people involved in the case – including the prime suspect. He urged the police officers to go and interview Bob and Ena his girlfriend. Bob and Ena had, by this time, split up, but Bob gave Whitehead Ena's address which he passed on to the police.

The detectives working on the case were unimpressed. Whitehead recalls, 'They were remarkably dismissive. Their attitude was, "Bob Brookes wasn't at the scene of the murder. What does he know?" '

This was not the only occasion Phillip Whitehead had gone sleuthing, come up with information, and met indifference when he attempted to hand over the fruits of his enquiries to the police.

He had earlier been involved in the curious affair of Keith Hibbert – the old lag in Leicester Jail to whom Michael Brookes had confided he, along with his stepson, had been involved in Lynn's murder.

Because of family complications, Hibbert was reluctant to tell his story. But his cellmate, an engaging criminal called Clive Shirtcliffe, was horrified that Michael Brookes appeared to be getting away with a brutal murder, and decided to do something about it.

He wrote a letter asking Phillip Whitehead to meet him. Again it was a strange rendezvous for a Member of Parliament going about his business – this time in a cell beneath the St Mary's Gate courtrooms in Derby.

Clive Shirtcliffe was on remand on a burglary charge. Whitehead secured permission from the court authorities, and went to see him. Shirtcliffe said that he had heard Michael Brookes confess to Hibbert that he had been involved in Lynn's murder. But the attitude of the police again was one of disinterest. 'He'll do or say anything to get a reduced sentence,' they said.

This time Whitehead kept up the pressure. The police did eventually go to see Keith Hibbert and secure a statement from him about his conversation with Brookes. A High Court judge said later that this was an important piece of evidence.

His role of amateur detective and his friendship with the Siddons family gave Phillip Whitehead a penetrating insight into Lynn's murder, the suspects, their families, and the police handling of the case, which he described as lamentable.

He raised the subject many times in Parliament. He discussed it in detail with the Attorney General, the late Michael Havers. Whitehead said, 'I can tell you he knew perfectly well there had been a massive miscarriage of justice here.'

Phillip Whitehead could have used parliamentary privilege to name Michael Brookes and accuse him of the murder without fear of recrimination. But he didn't. In all the times he referred to the case, he never mentioned Brookes by name.

There was a very good reason. He explained:

The real problem was to try to be fair to this wretched creature. If I had named him, there would have been a lot of headlines, but he would never have had a trial. The defence would say the jury had been prejudiced against their client, and he would have been acquitted instead of being put away for this terrible crime.

17   Voices from the Spirit World

Lynn Siddons never lived in the neat terraced house in Keldholme Lane, Alvaston which since 1985 has been her grandmother's home. But her presence there is sustained by all her possessions which Flo has saved and treasured with a zealous love.

There are pictures of Lynn in bathing costumes on holiday beaches. There are photographs of her playing with her cousins, her schoolfriends, and her black and white terrier, Lassie.

On the mantelpiece are rows of little ornaments and souvenirs she brought back from her trips. Models of farmyard animals, a plaster kitten, and one she was especially proud of, a fossilized sea urchin.

On holidays Lynn was always poking about in rock pools, and she found the fossil at Beer in Devon. She brought it home in her bag of trinkets and took it to the city museum in Derby where experts examined it and told her it was 200 million years old.

Her grandmother has a bedroom which she has virtually turned into a shrine to Lynn. The drawers and wardrobes are full of her things. Some of her clothes are there, including the black blazer she wore to school, the black-and-white striped tie and the spotless white blouse ... If the top button wasn't done up, it meant a stinging swish of the cane. There are old school reports, essay books, pads with funny childish drawings of animals and monsters.

Her record collection is there. Flo would never part with it. All the pop songs she used to play with her schoolfriends – Elvis Presley, Buddy Holly, The Everly Brothers and her favourite group for jiving to – Showaddywaddy

Flo says, 'Sometimes I go into that room, and I can smell

the perfume she used to wear. I feel almost able to reach out and touch her. I think about her every day, and I often dream about her at night.'

Often she flicks through Lynn's schoolbooks, and reads the essays and stories she wrote. She always got good marks for her compositions, which the teachers found imaginative and well-written.

In one of her books, she wrote a short essay entitled 'How we can help the poor'. Flo often reads it. It reminds her of how Lynn befriended old people, and helped them, even sharing her pocket money with some of them. Lynn wrote:

> I would like to help the poor by giving up sweets and comics which I like very much, and also if I had a lot of money, and take them for a holiday which none of them have really had, and buy them pretty clothes and save up leftover pocket money and for the old people I would like to buy them coal which some of them can't afford and good food to help them through the winter months and also warm clothing. My grandad is 85 and my grandma has died. She has been dead for 14 years, and I help him in what way I can. That is how I would like to help the poor.

Flo has consulted a number of mediums to try to make contact with Lynn through the spirit world, in the hope that the dead girl might say something that would help entrap her killers.

In 1985 she invited a medium called Ann Toogood from Burton-on-Trent to visit her. The woman came to her home knowing nothing of the murder. Flo handed her a gold ring which belonged to Lynn. Ann Toogood said:

> It all happened so quickly. I felt this pain as if somebody was stabbing me. Everything started to go black. I felt as if my head was going under water, and I was being strangled at the same time. With strong will I was able to break away from the violence. But I was still choking and needed a glass of water to help me recover. I was flabbergasted when I found out afterwards from her grandmother about the murder. It was an experience I would not want to go through again.

Flo also visited a male medium in Nottingham. She says, 'As soon as I went into his consulting room, he told me he could smell fish and chips. Fish and chips was Lynn's favourite meal ...'

But her strangest encounter with a medium was when the famous spiritualist Doris Collins visited Derby to give a demonstration of her powers. More than 1,600 people gathered in the Assembly Rooms to watch her. Flo was sitting near the front with two friends.

In her book *The Power Within* Doris Collins recalls:

> The story of Lynn Siddons revealed itself to me when I was in Derby. According to the local newspaper, more than 1600 people sat in stunned silence as this pretty sixteen-year-old girl who had been asphyxiated and stabbed thirty times with a knife seven years earlier in a copse at Barrow-on-Trent, Derby, came with a message for her grandmother who was present with two friends in the audience.

Doris Collins gave the background to the case, saying how Roy Brookes had been acquitted after making a statement blaming his stepfather who denied any involvement. She said, 'Following the jury's verdict clearing the young boy, Lynn's murder has remained the district's great unsolved murder case. I can understand therefore why the Derby audience was on tenterhooks when it became obvious to them that I had made contact with young Lynn Siddons.'

Doris then repeated her conversation with Lynn, saying:

> For what it is worth, she told me first there were two of us together. Exactly what this meant I do not know. She then spoke to me about grass and it is possible she was referring to some grass nearby the copse where she was left to die.
>
> 'They killed me,' she said, emphasising the pronoun. 'There were two. There were three at first and the other one left.'
>
> 'I don't know about that,' the grandmother said.
>
> 'I don't like saying this,' I told the grandmother. 'But I've got to repeat what she said.'
>
> 'They took me to pieces,' she said.
>
> 'Yes, that's true,' said the grandmother. 'That's true. They did.'
>
> 'I struggled and I fought and I knew I couldn't get away.

Neither of them have been caught. The other one didn't do anything.'

I take this last sentence perhaps to refer to the third person who went away.

Lynn told me that her murderers would have to come to justice. 'And I will see that they do,' she said. 'They shouldn't do things like that to people.'

'Did she sometimes call you Nan?' I asked, realising for the first time that the woman in the audience was probably the girl's grandmother.

'Sometimes.'

'Who's Florrie?' I asked.

'My name's Florence,' the lady said.

'Oh it's you. You're her grandma,' I said.

'Yes.'

'And who's Linda, or Lynn?'

'That's her name,' the grandmother said.

'Right,' I continued. 'Lynn shouted her name, Lynn, not Linda, and she said she wants you to know they are going to pay. She didn't tease them, she says. She wasn't like that. They were just determined to get her.'

Doris Collins continued:

'Now, I've got to be careful. It's almost as if I'm in the middle of a war. You won't half get it, she told me, because everybody knows who they are.'

'Everybody does!' the grandmother interjected.

And nobody does anything about it, the girl's telling me. 'Thank God, Doris. You've got the courage to come and stick up for me. They all know who they are and they don't do anything about it.'

I have to say that whatever this meant to Lynn's grandmother or the audience, it meant nothing to me. It certainly struck a chord with the audience because they started clapping furiously.

Addressing the grandmother again, I said 'Lynn says that the other mediums didn't know. Is that right?'

'Yes it is.'

She says that they were afraid, but I'm not. She says everybody knows but I don't know what she means, I concluded.

Lynn's grandmother has left no stone unturned in trying to bring the killer ... or killers ... to justice. She has tried more than once to reach Lynn with the help of spiritualists. But she was kind enough to say that her granddaughter's message through me was the most successful that had so far been obtained, and she was convinced from the details I provided that it was genuine.

Afterwards, Flo explained why she sought the help of spiritualists. She said:

I do believe in it to a certain degree. I just want to see if I can get through to Lynn and send a message to her. I would just like to ask her if she is all right now. I know how much she must have suffered. I would also like to find out if we will win our fight for justice. I sometimes wish for a miracle that Lynn would come to me in my sleep and tell me all that happened. But miracles don't happen, do they?

In spite of her forays into the spirit world, Flo was pursuing her down-to-earth campaign to get action against Lynn's killers with as much vigour and determination as ever. She took a part-time job as a cleaner to finance the travel, postage, telephone bills that kept mounting up as her fight continued.

She wrote letters to just about everyone she could think of. Dozens of MPs received pleas to support her cause in her clear rounded handwriting. She wrote to the Prime Minister, Home Secretary, Euro MPs, top lawyers, journalists – anybody who might be able to help her.

She says, 'Ever since Lynn's death, I've had difficulty sleeping properly. I'd get most of my ideas sitting up late at night. And then I'd have to act on them there and then. I must have written hundreds of letters. Sometimes I wrote to people two or three times. I was determined to get action.'

Throughout the long campaign, Flo was always alert to any opportunity to bring up Lynn's case. When the Home Secretary, Leon Brittan, visited Derby on 6 July 1985, a friend rang to say he was addressing a meeting at the Midland Hotel.

Never one to let a chance go by, she immediately rang Cynthia who drove around and picked her up. The pair of them went into the Midland Hotel. Flo was determined to see Leon Brittan and tell him, the country's main custodian of law and order, about the dangerous murderer who was still at large – the man who had killed Lynn.

Lynn aged three as a bridesmaid at her mother's wedding

Lynn as a young teenager, fooling about with her half-brother, Gary Halford

Lynn just after starting at St Thomas More School when she was eleven

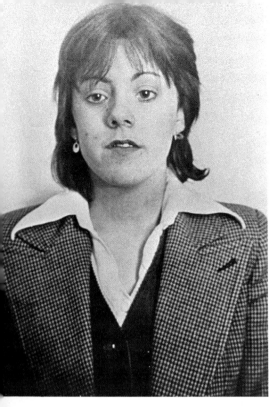

One of the last photographs of Lynn Siddons, which was taken a few weeks before her savage killing

Michael Brookes was interviewed on TV shortly after Lynn's murder. He denied killing her then, and has continued to do so ever since

Roy Brookes at the time of his trial for Lynn's murder. Though aged fifteen, he was described as having the mind and build of a 12-year-old

Dot Brookes, who signed a statement naming her husband as Lynn's killer and describing his perverted sexual practices

Lynn's family and their hundreds of supporters take to the streets demanding action over the unsolved crime

Chief Superintendent Jim Reddington, the detective in charge of the murder investigation which was severely criticized

Michael Brookes photographed outside his Peterborough home by a hidden camera team from the BBC

Phillip Whitehead, the Derby MP who became a friend of the Siddons family and who turned detective to gather evidence against Lynn's killers

Flo Siddons sits at home surrounded by pictures of her beloved granddaughter, including an oil painting hanging above the fireplace

Every month Flo Siddons and Gail make their sad pilgrimage to
Melbourne cemetery to put flowers in Lynn's memorial vase

After a campaign lasting nearly thirteen years, Flo, Gail and Cynthia
prepare for the High Court hearing

Campaigning journalist Paul Foot who first named Lynn's killers in print, in the *Daily Mirror,* outside the High court with Flo and Gail

Michael Brookes sporting his newly grown beard outside the Old Bailey during his trial in June 1996

Flo waited patiently in the hotel lobby for Mr Brittan to finish his private meeting. Then she pounced. She introduced herself, shook his hand, and pleaded with him to use his influence to get the case resolved.

Leon Brittan promised he would get the Attorney General to look again at the Lynn Siddons file, and consider any new evidence that had been put forward. Nothing came of it ... but as Flo says, 'He was very sympathetic and I'm sure he kept his word.'

Sympathy for the Siddons cause was growing every day. As the people of Derby realized the grave injustice Lynn's family had suffered, more and more of them pledged their support.

The case had been widely reported in the newspapers, and many of them were openly naming Michael Brookes as the man accused of Lynn's murder. The Press campaign was mounting. But it was from the ordinary people Flo and her family met in the streets that she derived most comfort. She says:

> Strangers would come up to me while I was shopping around the market or the city centre and ask, 'Are you Mrs Siddons? We've seen your picture in the newspaper.' Then they'd wish me well, and say 'More power to your elbow' or some other encouraging greeting.
>
> And the telephone used to ring all hours of the day or night. Again it was wellwishers offering help or advice. Everybody seemed to be on my side.

There was startling evidence of this before she left Sinfin to move to Alvaston and while she still lived in Carlyle Street. One night her house was burgled, and the thief, as well as taking cash and the TV set, stole the gold ring Lynn was wearing at the time of her death.

Flo appealed for its return through the local press. The ring was sent anonymously to the police with a note asking for it to be returned to the family.

Even the criminals of Derby were touched, it seemed, by the Lynn Siddons murder – and shocked, presumably, that her killer, though his name was well known, should still be free.

18   Enter the Press

Journalist Paul Foot needed a good strong item to lead his column in the *Daily Mirror*. In his notebook he had just the right story. He had been put on to it by an old university friend, the MP for Derby North, Phillip Whitehead. They had been at Oxford together where, curiously, Whitehead, though now a Labour MP, was chairman of the University Conservative Association.

Whitehead had telephoned Foot and said, 'There's something going on up here that you should look into.' It was the Lynn Siddons murder – and the campaign to bring her killers to justice by her family.

Foot was so intrigued he invited Flo and Gail to visit him in London. He took them into his fourth floor office at the headquarters of *Mirror* Group Newspapers overlooking Holborn Circus and listened fascinated as their story poured out.

Yes, it was the perfect item to lead his weekly page, and after checking the story by making a number of phone calls, he sat down at his typewriter and wrote it.

A controversial column like Foot's has to be read by lawyers before publication. The Lynn Siddons story had hardly left his hands before the head of the *Mirror*'s legal department, a barrister called Hugh Corrie, appeared at his door holding the copy with a worried frown on his face. 'I'm sorry Paul, I can't pass this story. It's absolutely impossible to publish an article like this.'

This was early in 1981, and although Foot had been writing his *Mirror* column for a couple of years, this was the first time the legal eagles (as the lawyers' department was known) had given any of his stories the thumbs down.

'Why not?' he asked, surprised and a little miffed.

'You'll never get it in. You just can't go round naming murderers who have not been convicted.'

Corrie explained that somewhere in the country an opportunist solicitor would be waiting poised to pounce on the item, offer to represent Michael and Roy Brookes, and make a fortune by claiming libel damages from the *Mirror*. Foot says:

> I knew I was sticking my neck out, but I did think the evidence was very strong. I thought it was something we ought to be able to get in. I sulked about it and made a fuss. I had to write some other story to take its place. It was a fifth rate story and a fifth rate column and I was not at all happy about it.

Hugh Corrie went back to his office but he did not dismiss the subject from his mind. He liked and admired Foot, and the last thing he wanted to do was to discourage him by killing a story Foot was keen to publish.

A week or so later, the lawyer appeared again in Foot's office. He wanted to talk about the Siddons murder. He and Foot discussed the complexities of the case for an hour or more.

Then Corrie said, 'Look, if you set out all the legal documentation, and you're careful not to make an absolute allegation that these men did the murder, I'll look at it again. If you set it out in greater detail and check everything once more, we might be able to get it in.'

Foot was delighted, and he set to work with vigour. There was another reason for his happy mood. He had just been nominated Campaigning Journalist of the Year, and a story like this, breaking new ground by naming an unconvicted murderer in print, would set the seal on the award.

His story, under the headline 'Who Killed Lynn Siddons?' was published on 8 April 1981, just a week after Lynn's Aunt Cynthia had appeared in court for driving her car at Michael and Dot Brookes.

Foot wrote, 'This is the background to the grim story which refuses to go away' and his article, when completed and laid out, covered two full pages of his newspaper. He set it out just as Hugh Corrie had advised in three long sections.

The first was the acquittal of Roy Brookes at his

Nottingham trial after he had blamed his stepfather for the murder saying his own small part in it had been done under duress.

The second section was the statement Dot Brookes made describing how knives played a part in their sex life and claiming Michael had admitted to her that he had stabbed Lynn. Dot made this statement to the police, but retracted it after Michael returned to live with her.

Foot rang her up and asked her why she had retracted the statement. He recorded her answer which was, 'I don't want to go into this now. I was not jealous of my husband as some people think. All I will say is you have to fight fire with fire, and that's what I did.'

She refused to enlarge on this, but there was no denial of her original statement – or her claim that Michael had admitted to her that he murdered Lynn.

When Foot played his tape of Dot Brookes' words to the *Mirror*'s chief lawyer, Corrie was impressed. Foot says, 'That was one of the things that helped to get my story into the paper.'

The third section covered the statements of Keith Hibbert and Clive Shirtcliffe, who had come forward following Flo Siddons' appeal for fresh evidence with a statement that Michael Brookes had admitted his involvement in Lynn's murder in a Derby pub.

The lawyers passed the story, and it was handed to the *Mirror*'s features editor, Richard Stott, who went on to become editor. Stott, says Foot, absolutely loved the story, and took personal charge of laying it out as a double page spread instead of the single page usually allocated to Foot's column.

The job was finished by mid afternoon on the Tuesday before publication. The words had all been checked, and everything fitted neatly into place. Foot and Stott had worked together all day and both were highly pleased with the result.

'It looks great,' said Stott. 'Come on, let's go and have a drink. We've earned it.'

As the two men set off to a wine bar called the Bottle Scrue just around the corner from their office, a proof of the Lynn Siddons spread was being taken by a messenger up to the ninth-floor office of the chairman of *Mirror* Group Newspapers, Tony Miles.

Miles, a former editor of the paper, nearly had an apoplectic fit when he saw it. His hand snaked out to the telephone. He demanded to see Stott instantly. But he was told the features editor had gone for a celebratory drink with the writer.

From his window, Miles could look down and see the Bottle Scrue. His fury mounted as far below he saw two tiny but recognizable figures, the perpetrators of this outrage, entering the bar. Before Stott and Foot had time to order their first drink, the phone rang.

It was Miles. He said to Stott, 'Have you two gone stark staring mad? We can't possibly put this into the paper. It will have to be pulled out. Come on back and put something else in.'

Stott and Foot returned to the office and took the lift to the chairman's office, collecting Hugh Corrie on the way. Miles was still fuming. He thought his prize campaigner, his features editor and his chief legal adviser had all taken leave of their senses.

Foot recalls, 'It took a long time – we must have been arguing for an hour or more – but eventually we were able to persuade him that the story should go in. But he was still very uneasy about it.'

Curiously, the chairman's wife was at the Savoy Hotel two days later when Foot went to collect his Campaigning Journalist award. She said to him, 'That was a great story. It was like a whodunnit. And I know who did the murder. The names are there.'

The story was not challenged by the Brookes or their lawyers, even though, as Foot says, if he had got it wrong it would be a horrendous libel. To call somebody a murderer is just about the worst possible thing you can call them, but as well as checking all of his facts, Foot felt strongly that printing the story was justified in the public interest. He recalls:

It was an unusual story in many ways. You had the incompetence of the police, the battle for justice by this very determined family, but most of all you had a murder where everybody knew the suspects but they were still free.

Most of my campaigning stories in the past had been to free people who had been wrongly convicted. But this was just as important – these people had committed a murder and appeared to be getting away with it. Nobody had been convicted because the police messed it up.

I still to this day can't comprehend how it was the Derbyshire police behaved so incredibly badly. The least they could do is say they made a mistake and charge the guy. If a jury finds him not guilty at the end of the day that's bad luck, but they could then say they'd done their job.

Paul Foot says that the factor that most influenced him in pursuing the Lynn Siddons story was the quiet determination of her grandmother. Since that first meeting, he and Flo Siddons have become friends, and many times she has rung him up, at his office and at his home, to tell him about the latest twists and turns in the case. He says:

She is a remarkable woman, quiet and humble but what an immense determination. Sometimes when you take up a case for someone they can become a bit of a menace, ringing you all the time with unimportant details. But Flo was never like this.

She was marvellous. In spite of her humility, she was exceedingly persistent. She obviously had faith in what I was doing and what the paper was doing. I found this very touching. Many of the people who come to me feel they have been let down by the authorities. In Florence's case, she had lost her loved one, and she felt the Derbyshire police had let her down.

A young girl had been cruelly murdered. Everybody knew who had done the murder. It was perfectly obvious who had done the murder. The police knew who had done the murder. The jury knew, the judge knew at Nottingham Crown Court. Everybody knew. And yet the man was walking around the streets.

It's worth making the point that people like myself who write about injustice are often accused of not being interested in the victims of crime. This case is an example of the opposite. Injustice can work both ways. It can work by the wrong people being convicted. And it can work by the right people not being convicted. It's a pernicious thing that a murderer can walk the streets free, and the Siddons family put their trust and faith in me to do something about it.

Paul Foot has returned to the story many times since he first broke it with that momentous spread. He said, 'What I wanted more than anything was for the Siddons family to be satisfied by the legal identification of Michael Brookes as Lynn's murderer. They had come to me after failing to get action from the police, and I was so impressed with them I was determined to help all I could.'

Like many people who have studied the case, Foot believes the fundamental error the police made was not their failure to prosecute anybody, but the speed with which they prosecuted the wrong person in the first place. He said:

> That is the terrible mistake they made, and I think it is a mistake police forces very often make. They get a certain amount of evidence, in this case a confession, and they don't bother to check the case any more than that.
>
> They've got the confession. They've got that the chap was out for a walk and says he knifed the girl. The girl was knifed to death – and that was enough for a conviction, so they leave the case on one side.
>
> When it turns out the confession itself is completely bogus, they didn't know what to do. When Roy Brookes was found not guilty, they were inclined to think they would look right wallies if, as soon as it became apparent the man who they tried to convince the court had done the murder had not done the murder – but somebody else had done the murder who was their chief prosecution witness. If they brought the chief prosecution witness in another murder trial, they would look complete idiots.

The press, he says, has fulfilled an important function in the Lynn Siddons case which the police failed to do. Lynn was murdered – it has been said many times – by a man with a lust for stabbing, a pervert who achieved a kind of sexual pleasure by plunging the knife repeatedly into her body. Killers who get this kind of pleasure will often kill and kill again if they can get away with it.

By identifying Lynn's killer, the press made sure he didn't get away with it – and possibly saved the life, or even lives, of potential future victims.

Foot says, 'This is very important. We did this – the media. It means that if a girl is touched anywhere in the area, the police are down on Brookes like a ton of bricks.

The publicity has rendered him impotent, and probably saved people from harm by him.'

Once Paul Foot had paved the way, as it were, by naming Michael and Roy Brookes as Lynn's killers, other newspapers and magazines followed, and Flo Siddons quickly realized that, in the media, she had a strong ally in her campaign for justice.

Writers from British and foreign magazines, television and radio reporters beat a path to her neat terraced house in Alvaston to interview the amazing little granny, and her daughters, who were battling against the authorities to avenge Lynn's death.

Every time a reporter or TV producer called, Flo got into the habit of writing down their telephone numbers in a book she keeps where everyone who has helped in the campaign is listed – with office address, home address and home and office telephone numbers if she can get them.

Some of the media representatives like Paul McCrea from the BBC have become good friends. Macrea had a special interest in the Lynn Siddons murder. His sister, Anne, went to the St Thomas More School and knew Lynn. As a Derby boy, he realised the immense and intense local interest in the case.

McCrea has produced several documentaries on the murder and the campaign. Like many of the reporters on Flo's list, he got into the habit of ringing her every week or so as a check to see if there were any new developments.

The *Derby Evening Telegraph* was just as aware of the degree of local concern that Lynn's killer had never been convicted. Over the thirteen years from her death to the High Court case against the Brookes, the paper published stories on average every two months making sure every new twist was fully covered.

An executive of the paper wrote to Gail Halford's solicitor, 'Public interest in the case is still very much alive, and people are concerned the murderer is still at large.'

Raymonds News Agency covers the Derby area for the national press. One of their directors, John Twells, a highly experienced journalist in the city with his ear very much to the ground, also confirmed the degree of public interest in Lynn's case, and he told Gail's solicitor that senior police

officers had confided in him their opinion that the wrong
man had been charged.

As well as writing about the case many times, Paul Foot
was able to do another service for Lynn's family. He had
seen, and written about, how they appeared to be banging
their heads against a brick wall without making much
progress. And he had an idea.

He knew a young idealistic and energetic solicitor in
practice in London. She was the sort of investigative lawyer
who would work night and day to correct an injustice. Her
name was Jane Deighton. Foot thought she was just the
person to get the Siddons case moving forward – and he
decided to introduce her to the family.

19   An Official Complaint

Six years had elapsed since Lynn Siddons was murdered and, as far as her family were aware, nothing was being done, by the police or anybody else, to bring her killers to justice.

Almost everybody around Derby knew who they were. Their names had been printed on posters and in newspapers and magazines. But they were still free to walk the streets, even though they had been driven from the city by the Siddons' hate campaign.

It was the apparent inactivity of the police that Flo Siddons found particularly galling. With simple logic, she asked herself: A girl has been murdered. The police know who killed her. Why has nobody been arrested?

Why indeed! To Flo and her family, the situation was intolerable. They had not been happy with the way the police had handled the case ever since those first days of Lynn's disappearance when officers kept insisting she had run away but would soon come back home.

The police had not sent a representative to Lynn's funeral. Flo says, 'That upset us very much. There always seems to be a detective or a uniformed officer at the funeral of murder victims – it's the police's way of paying their respects and showing the family they care. But nobody from the police came to Lynn's funeral. Why, we just don't know.'

Then there was the mislaying of the knife and partly burnt clothing found in the garden after Mick Brookes and his family moved away from Carlyle Street.

At first the Siddons family put it down to negligence. But it began to cross their minds that there might be a more sinister reason. Could it be that these items had been deliberately lost to save the police the embarrassment of staging a second trial – and admitting their mistake of charging the wrong person in the first place?

By their own efforts the family had traced witnesses whom the police had never been to see. They had discovered Mick Brookes' brother Bob had tried to give a statement to the police, but no officer bothered to write it down.

Some of these things may have been important, others less so. But to the Siddons family they all added up to a massive botch by the law, compounded by the alarming and indisputable fact that Lynn's killers were still free.

Flo decided that something must be done about this unfortunate catalogue of errors. In December 1984, she went to see a county councillor called Harry Lowe, a member of the police committee, who helped her draft an official complaint – under Section 49 of the 1964 Police Act – against Derbyshire police for their mishandling of the Lynn Siddons murder investigation.

According to the rules, she had to name a name. And the name she put in her letter of complaint, dated 25 October 1984, was the name of the officer who was in charge of the investigation, Detective Superintendent James Reddington.

Derbyshire at this time had an Acting Chief Constable, Alan Smith. There is a procedure for handling complaints against a police officer which he immediately put into operation, calling in another force, in this case Merseyside, to investigate the complaint.

Early in 1985 two officers from Merseyside – Assistant Chief Constable Ernest Miller and Det Chief Inspector Bill Coady – arrived in Derby to begin their probe.

Policemen never like the job of investigating charges against their brother officers. It's an irksome but necessary duty that occasionally they have to face. Miller and Coady, two highly experienced officers from the tough training ground of Liverpool, went about their business determined to expose any shortcomings in the Derbyshire investigation, but with a minimum of fuss.

Their investigation took six months. At the end of that time, they produced their report. It was in three sections. The first, running to sixty pages, contained their findings and recommendations. The second, about fifty pages long, consisted of the statements they had taken from witnesses.

The third, again about fifty pages, comprised other documents to back up their findings. The bulky report was handed to the Acting Chief Constable.

The report has never been made public, in spite of efforts by Derbyshire councillors, notably David Bookbinder, to make it so. But it is believed to have been highly critical – some people say severely critical – of the way Derbyshire police conducted the murder inquiry.

The report completely exonerated Superintendent Reddington of any negligence allegations. He conducted his duties by the book. Indeed, Flo Siddons only put his name to the complaint as a tactic because under the Police Complaints Procedures she had to. What she wanted investigated was the force – not Jim Reddington.

And the Merseyside officers did just as she wished, even though they could have stopped their probe as soon as they had dealt with Reddington's part in the investigation. That was all they were briefed to do, but off their own bat they did more.

As well as covering the ground Derbyshire police had been over and reinterviewing many of the witnesses Derbyshire detectives had seen, the Merseyside duo wanted to see whether the investigation could be taken any further.

Any recommendations they made have remained secret just like their criticisms of Derbyshire police. But it is believed they recommended that an outside force should take over the murder investigation and try to build up a case to take Mick Brookes to trial. This recommendation was not acted upon.

The Merseyside detectives spoke to new witnesses, including Carol Dunworth – the woman Brookes ran away with when he left Dot. She was present when police arrested Brookes in the caravan where they were living together at Skegness. But for some reason Derbyshire police never interviewed her, even though she claimed Brookes had admitted to her that he attacked Lynn.

This and other new evidence uncovered by the Merseyside detectives was presented to the Director of Public Prosecutions. But again he decided it was not sufficiently strong to warrant putting Michael Brookes on trial.

The debate about whether the Merseyside report should,

or should not, be made public simmered on well into 1985. On 22 October that year, David Bookbinder, the controversial Labour leader of the county council, raised it at a meeting of Derbyshire Police Authority.

He had done so, he said, at the request of Florence Siddons and her family. Flo, Gail and her husband John, Cynthia and Keith were at the meeting in the County Hall at Matlock where David Bookbinder raised four points:

1. The inquiry by Merseyside Police has been completed. The national press, in the form of Paul Foot of the Mirror, claimed that Derbyshire police were severely criticised in various parts of this inquiry. Will the Acting Chief Constable confirm or deny that Derbyshire police were criticised?

2. Is the murder inquiry continuing? If the file is still open, is the police view that they will bring it to a conclusion in the not too distant future?

3. Is the whole of the report, in view of the public concern, to be made public?If to do so would frustrate continuing police inquries, tell us.

4. If it cannot be published, in view of the deep concern of Mrs Siddons and her family, is it possible under the tightest confidentiality for them to see the result of their complaint? If it had been a court of law there would have been a transcript. I know it is Mrs Siddons' express will to have a sight of it, and she would accept confidentiality.

Replying, Alan Smith said, 'I know I speak for all members of the Derbyshire constabulary in extending my sympathy to Mrs Siddons and her family. Everything humanly possible is being done to resolve this inquiry.'

These words cut no ice with Flo Siddons sitting in the public gallery. Sympathy? Why had no police officer represented the force at Lynn's funeral? Everything humanly possible being done? Why can't murderers be arrested when the police know who they are?

Alan Smith said Mrs Siddons' complaint was that the officer in charge of the case had not carried out his duties properly. Following the investigation by the Merseyside officers, a report that the complaint was not substantiated went to the Police Complaints Authority.

A second part of the Merseyside report on the murder inquiry was examined by the Police Complaints Authority.

They came to the decision that it did not reveal any evidence of any disciplinary offences committed by officers of the Derbyshire constabulary.

Mr Smith said the investigation was not closed, and the Director of Public Prosecutions had been fully consulted about every development. But he did say that Mrs Siddons and her family could not see the report.

Even now Flo Siddons has never seen the report that resulted from her complaint. Nor has the public. Not even members of the Police Authority were allowed to see it. Only a few very senior police officers were given this privilege.

David Bookbinder still thinks this is wrong. He told me:

> Even if it was critical of the police, it should have been published. Keeping it secret leaves a fog over the whole issue.
>
> If it was felt parts of the report might prejudice a future trial, then the police could have hired a lawyer to produce a summary of the report so that those parts that the public ought to know about could be released. It is very unsatisfactory just leaving things as they were.
>
> In the public interest and in the police interest, the report should be made public. There are so many unanswered questions. It leaves a nasty taste in the mouth.

Even though the Merseyside report has remained securely locked in a safe in the Chief Constable's office at Derbyshire police headquarters at Butterley Hall in Ripley, it is not difficult for those with a sound knowledge of police procedures to speculate on its likely contents.

I have discussed the Lynn Siddons murder with many senior police officers in different parts of the country, and they have given me their assessment of where the Derbyshire police went wrong.

One officer, a detective superintendent in a large bustling northern city, who gave his opinion, has been involved in more than fifty murder investigations. He said:

> The trouble with these country bumpkin police forces is they only get a handful of murders every year, where big forces are dealing with two or three a week. It's quite possible that some of the officers investigating Lynn Siddons' death had

never been involved in a murder investigation before. They just aren't up to it. They haven't the experience.

Police officers I spoke to were appalled that Michael Brookes was allowed to have ten minutes alone with Roy on the night of the arrest. That lapse produced a false confession upon which the whole shaky case was based, and everything started going wrong from that moment.

This came about because of the Judges Rules which state that when a juvenile is being questioned by the police, there should be an independent person present. This would explain why Michael Brookes was allowed to be present. But as a principal witness against Roy, he should never have been allowed to spend time alone with him.

Experienced detectives tell me there were two other horrendous gaffes by the Derbyshire police that night in Pear Tree police station when Roy Brookes was being questioned.

The first was his statement – it covered just one sheet of paper. The usual police procedure is to wring everything you can from a murder suspect. The statement should cover pages and pages – not just a brief account of his version of how he committed the crime.

A senior police officer gave me the reason for this. He said:

Only by getting down masses of detail leading up to the crime, the crime itself, and what happened afterwards can you begin to corroborate a murder statement. If your suspect travelled to the scene of the crime by double decker bus and sat next to a lady in a red raincoat, all that needs to be written down. You then find the lady in the red raincoat, and she corroborates your suspect's story that he was on the bus.

But there was none of this in Roy Brookes' terse statement. There was no peripheral detail for the police to check and test so they would have an idea as to whether the kernel of the statement was itself true.

The second procedural mistake, even more serious, was to charge Roy Brookes before the detailed forensic report was available. Dr Usher was still doing his work on Lynn's body at the time the boy was charged.

Commenting on this, my police contact said:

It's unbelievable. You need these forensic details to check against the story your suspect is telling. You need to be able to question him about the number of stab wounds, the soil in the mouth, all of those things. There was no hurry to charge this youth. They could have kept him for as long as they liked. To me it looks as if some of those police officers were in a great hurry to wrap up the job and get away. They were not painstaking and thorough as detectives have to be when they are dealing with murder inquiries.

Derbyshire police admitted they moved Lynn's body before carrying out the usual forensic tests. You don't need to be a policeman to know this is a fundamental error. In detective stories on TV, one of the first questions is, 'Has anybody touched the body?' Derbyshire police didn't just touch it – they carried it away.

In fact, it was left to the Merseyside detectives many years later to carry out some of these basic tests. They knew they had to get some forensic evidence to back up Roy Brookes' statement. One of the clues in his description of the killing was that Michael Brookes had used his foot to press Lynn's face into a puddle of water.

The Merseyside officers contacted Professor Alan Usher at his Sheffield Laboratory and were relieved to find he still had the samples he had taken from Lynn's body six years previously – including her lungs. He was able to get a tiny drop of water from her lungs which was compared under a high-powered microscope with samples of water taken from the banks of the canal.

Water contains microscopic growths of algae, known as diatoms which vary according to the source of the sample. The diatoms in the water taken from Lynn's lungs contained identical diatoms to the samples taken from the canal.

Diatom identification is not, like fingerprints, a positive indicator. But this new discovery did show that Lynn had inhaled water of broadly the same type as that found in the canal. It may not have been a conclusive piece of evidence, but it did help to support the truth of part of Roy Brookes' statement.

Another more obvious mistake was in the Derbyshire police not asking themselves how could a puny, under-developed weakling, fifteen years old but looking more like twelve, overpower, strangle, stab and drag away the body of a taller, stronger, heavier victim.

A police contact said, 'It's hardly a three-pipe problem for Sherlock Holmes. It must have been obvious to anyone just looking at him that this lad could not have done what he said he did alone and unaided. So who helped him? The stepfather should have been under suspicion from the very beginning.'

There is another possible explanation for the way Derbyshire police mishandled the Lynn Siddons investigation in those vital early stages where mistakes set the seal on the whole bungled case.

Until 1 April 1967 Derby City had its own police force and so did Derbyshire county. The two forces were amalgamated. But according to officers I have spoken to the traditional rivalry between them lingered on for many years after the merger.

The theory has been put forward that groups of detectives from both city and county were involved in Lynn's murder inquiry – and the former city officers wanted to show their county cousins how speedily they could wrap up the case and lock up the prisoner.

A police officer told me, 'It was like rivalry between schools or army regiments, and the former city officers wanted to be able to say "My regiment is better than yours".'

True, they did say, 'We've got him. We've done the job.' But in their haste they locked up the wrong person – a mistake that was to haunt them down the years.

20　Through the Legal Jungle

By the end of 1985 and after one more refusal, the fourth, by the Director of Public Prosecutions to hold a fresh trial for the murder of Lynn Siddons, her family were fed up with the law – and lawyers.

They had paid a hefty legal bill a year or so previously, and they couldn't afford to get involved any more with solicitors – especially as all they had received from the Criminal Injuries Board as compensation for Lynn's death was a paltry cheque for £27. Flo said:

> I was disgusted. I almost decided to send it back. That was the price they put on a young girl's life.
>
> All the campaigning, seeing lawyers and journalists in London, meeting Members of Parliament, was costing more than I could afford, even though all the family were helping to pay the bills. I estimate the fight to get justice for Lynn has cost me more than £14,000.

When Paul Foot offered to put them in touch with a solicitor who, he said, might be able to help them, they were, at first, a little apprehensive. But Foot said, 'She'll do it for nothing, or at least she'll try to get you legal aid. She's very good and extremely dedicated. Give it a go. I'm sure she'll help you.'

Right from the start, Jane Deighton was not only intrigued with the case, but appalled that a young girl had been murdered, and her killers, although their names were known, still at large. She was even more appalled at the total lack of activity by the authorities.

She set out the problem this way:

A murder one would expect to be a criminal case. But Mrs Siddons has tried to persuade the police to prosecute. She's tried to persuade the Director of Public Prosecutions to prosecute. And they simply won't do it.

Now, of course, theoretically, she could bring a private prosecution for murder. But the system just prevents her from doing that. A private prosecution would be fantastically expensive. Anyone wanting to bring a private prosecution would have to be very, very wealthy, and Mrs Siddons isn't wealthy.

Secondly, if she did bring a private prosecution, it would be open to the DPP to take it over and do with that prosecution what they wanted. It's quite clear that what they would do is to take it over and stop it.

There were other complications – Roy Brookes had been tried for murder, and acquitted. Could he be tried a second time for the same offence, even if the charge was brought privately?

And there was the legal problem about evidence from accomplices. If Michael Brookes was charged with murder, would the evidence of the one and only eye witness, his stepson Roy, be acceptable as Roy had admitted playing a part, albeit under duress, in the murder?

All these difficulties added up to a huge conundrum, a seemingly impenetrable legal barrier, where laws of evidence and Judge's Rules were intertwined like jungle creepers blocking the path to justice.

But Jane Deighton, who according to Paul Foot has a brilliantly innovative legal brain, probed and prodded at the problem, first looking at it one way, then another, until she thought she had found a possible way through.

Instead of initiating a private prosecution for murder, she had a novel idea … to take a civil action against Michael and Roy Brookes for battery and to seek damages from them for causing Lynn's death.

It would be the first time in the history of British law that a pair of killers had been brought before the courts by their accusers in this way, and ahead Jane Deighton could see many obstacles. Undaunted, she set her course, and launched herself upon it with an iron determination to win justice for her clients.

The first of the obstacles was money. Going to law is a costly business and somebody would have to pick up the bills. Deighton decided to apply for legal aid for the Siddons family to pay for the barrister's fees, her own costs and the heavy expenses of rushing round the country to interview witnesses and build up the case.

Twice Flo Siddons and Gail Halford had to go to London for meetings with the Law Society officials who would make the decision on their application for legal aid.

One of their allies was the MP for Derby North, Greg Knight, who, like his predecessor in the constituency, Phillip Whitehead, felt that the case of Lynn Siddons had gone on for far too long.

Mr Knight said, 'I'm writing to the Law Society urging them to grant Legal Aid on the basis that the case is one of regional importance.'

At the headquarters of the Law Society in Chancery Lane, Flo and Gail listened to the interminable discussions among lawyers, and watched the masses of files and documents being passed around. Then they were asked to wait outside. They were told they would have to wait a few days for the decision to be sent to them by post.

But Flo already knew what those august figures had decided. After the meeting one of them took pity on her and whispered as he passed her in the corridor, 'It's all right. You're going to get your legal aid. Don't say who told you, but I couldn't bear the thought of you being on tenterhooks while you waited to hear formally.'

Before striding off to join his fellow lawyers, he gripped Flo's arm and said, 'Good luck with your case.'

The official confirmation came a few days later in the usual large buff envelope. The good news, which Flo already knew, was that the application for legal aid had been granted. But there was some bad news, too. The money the state would provide would not cover all the costs. It left a shortfall which Flo and her family would have to make up.

All her savings had already gone on her expenses waging the campaign against Lynn's murderers. She was having to scrimp as it was. When she and Gail went to London for their meetings with lawyers and officials, they got up especially early to catch a train which left Derby at 5.31 a.m.

because it was cheaper than the later rush hour trains. They gave up part of their sleep to economize on travel.

The first instalment of the legal aid payments was £500, and, with help from her family, supporting her as always, Flo managed to pay this. She was earning a little money with her part-time cleaning job in the evenings, and that helped towards the bill.

Then came a shock. She was told by Jane Deighton that another £1,500 was needed. No way could the family pay this. So Flo got in touch with one of her newspaper friends and an appeal was published for help to meet the legal bills for the campaign.

The appeal did not ask directly for money. That would be a bit like begging, and Flo's pride would never allow her to beg for help. She asked people to support functions, and assist with sponsored events, to see if the money could be raised that way.

The death of Lynn Siddons was an emotive subject in Derby, and the city people opened their hearts. Scores of friends took out sponsorship forms, gave raffle prizes, helped to organize a jumble sale and do other less conventional acts to help the Siddons family.

One of the events was a sponsored walk along the twenty-mile road from Derby to Matlock. The dozen walkers met at the Market Place on 13 March 1988. It was a poignant choice of date – Mothering Sunday – so Lynn was very much to the fore of Flo's thoughts. The cold rain lashed down unkindly as the walkers set out.

Gail was there, along with Cynthia and Keith. Even Flo, though seventy-three years old, strode bravely through the puddles. But the walk proved too much for her. After doing eight miles along the A6, she had to give up near Keith's home in Belper. But the rest carried on, raising hundreds of pounds.

The bric a brac stall the family organized the following Friday afternoon at Allenton Market was another success. At the end of the sale all the trinkets and clothes they had been given were cleared, and they had another £200 in the kitty.

Lynn's friend from the next street, Pat Edmunds, hunted through her cupboards and found a bottle of Scotch which she gave as a raffle prize. A woman came up to Flo in the street and gave her an envelope containing £5. People were knocking at her door with money and raffle prizes. One cheque arrived with a 'Good Luck' message written on the back. It was for £100.

Three regulars at the Silver Ghost public house in Alvaston thought of an unusual way to make some money for the appeal – and have a laugh at the same time.

Andy Meehan, Carl Meehan and Nick Gilsenan ate a meal of daffodil heads followed by raw eggs which they washed down with beer and spirits. They were feeling pretty groggy, but each of them managed to do twenty press-ups afterwards. Customers were so impressed with the zany stunt they contributed £350.

When she first heard that £1,500 would be needed, Flo thought getting the money would be a daunting prospect. But in three weeks, that sum had been exceeded. Flo gave a grateful comment, 'It's wonderful. Everyone has been so helpful. This proves the people of Derby are behind us.'

And Gail added her thanks. She said, 'Lynn was murdered ten years ago. It's a long time for people to remember. Not her family and friends, of course. We think of her every day. But this response shows people have not forgotten. It's been hard work organizing everything, but the Derby people have been so good.'

It may not have taken long to raise the money, but the wheels of justice still turned slowly. It was on 1 April 1987 that a writ was issued by Jane Deighton on behalf of Gail and Florence claiming damages from Michael and Roy Brookes – but they were to wait two years before the case came before the courts.

The writ set out the events of that fateful day – 3 April 1978 – that Lynn died, and said she had gone walking with Fitzroy, then only fifteen, along the banks of the Trent Canal near Sinfin, when they were joined by Fitzroy's stepfather, Michael Brookes. It said:

Michael Brookes then attacked the deceased from behind and held her around the neck. They both then variously stabbed the deceased using a carving knife and a sheath knife.

Michael then attempted to asphyxiate the deceased by compressing her neck, pushing soil into her mouth and pressing her face into a pool of water. He dragged the body into undergrowth and left her. It is Mrs Halford's case that this was a brutal and sexually perverted murder, committed at the instigation of Michael Brookes. In particular, the deceased's body was mutilated by eleven tiny knife tip wounds immediately above the navel and by four major stab wounds and nine tiny knife tip penetrations immediately above the pubis.

There were in excess of 40 knife wounds to her body together with other injuries. The deceased suffered agonizing pain and terror before she finally lost consciousness and died.

The bill for damages was set out as follows:

Item: To causing the victim agonizing pain and terror before she lost consciousness and died   Cost Unknown

Item: Lost income due to death. Deceased was due to start work as a meat packer for the Central Midlands Co-op at a gross wage of £40 a week. The said wages would have increased in stages to a 1986 level of £80.75 a week

Cost Unknown

Item: Funeral expenses	£177.85
Tombstone	£13. 82

Item: A gross affront to the physical integrity and dignity of an innocent young girl of 16

Aggravated and exemplary damages.

Item: Damages under the Law Reform Act 1934.

Item: Interest under Section 35A of the Supreme Court Act 1981.

When it reported the High Court hearing, the *Derby Evening Telegraph* gave the whole of its front page to this unique document under the headline: 'Your bill, Mr Brookes'.

The account for Lynn's death had been presented. But the question remained: Would it ever be paid?

21   One Door Shuts – Another Opens

Tears do not come easily to Flo Siddons. She feels deeply, but a hard upbringing disciplined her not to show her feelings. She tends to be gently disparaging of people who cry too readily. But she was reduced to sobbing at a decision of the courts in 1989.

After a succession of minor victories in the long struggle to bring Lynn's killers to justice, a sudden defeat had come crashing down. It stood before her, what seemed like an insurmountable barrier to further progress, and the tears trickled down her face.

The date was 22 November. With Gail and Cynthia at her side she stood in the large square in front of the High Court at Manchester. She had just heard Mr Justice Schiemann bar her from pursuing her claim for damages against Roy and Michael Brookes. It seemed so final at the end of her long battle.

An action for damages, which is what Florence and Gail were seeking on behalf 'of the estate of Lynn Siddons', normally has to be started within three years of the attack.

But a judge has the discretion, in certain circumstances, to disapply the three-year rule, and to allow the action to go ahead even if it is outside the time limit.

In the Siddons case, it was five-and-a-half years beyond the limit, and after hearing arguments that the Brookes would not be able to pay damages, and any court hearing would not be fair to them, Mr Justice Schiemann gave his ruling.

He said that the case was 'financially pointless' adding, 'The problems here arise from the probability that the defendants will not have sufficient assets to meet any judgements which might be given against them.'

Mr Justice Schiemann also said it would be 'clearly prejudicial to the defendants' to have new evidence on the case called such a long time after Lynn's death. Witnesses memories would have clouded, and the publicity could prevent a fair trial.

Outside the court Cynthia told waiting reporters, 'It is frustrating when you think of everything we've gone through. We keep getting somewhere, then the door shuts in our face. Sometimes it's like hitting your head against a brick wall because you don't seem to be getting anywhere.'

Gail, too, was asked for her views. She said, 'We were hoping it was going to go our way. But we've got used to suffering disappointments over the years. It's still not going to stop us. We'll still carry on.'

Perhaps because of the tears, Flo was not asked for her comment. But when she got home she wrote in her diary, 'The Judge kept talking about limitation periods. He could have overruled. But he didn't. We had the wrong judge. We want Brookes in prison where he should have been years ago. We won't stop until we get what we've been fighting for – good old British justice. But this is now being made a mockery of.'

However, the battling Siddons did not mope for long. They soon came up with other ideas for pursuing their campaign. No way were they going to allow the opinion of one judge to deflect them after their long and bitter struggle, sometimes within the law, sometimes outside it.

Gail said:

> We're very angry he took such a narrow-minded view of the case. He should have had the guts to stick his neck out and waive the time limit rule. There was more than enough evidence to support the case going ahead.
>
> We have come too far to give up now. We will go to the Court of Appeal, the European Court of Human Rights, or wherever it takes to bring Lynn's killer to justice.

Flo took up her pen again, and began to write letters. One of the first was to the Euro MP, Geoffrey Hoon, to see if the case could be pursued through the European Courts. She also wrote to the Lord Chancellor, Lord Hailsham. She wrote again to the Derbyshire police asking why Lynn's killers, when they were known, were allowed to remain at large.

Her letter to the police resulted in a visit from the Chief Constable Alan Smith with his CID head, Chief Supt Bailey. Mr Smith assured her the case was reviewed every three months. Flo wrote in her diary, 'I took this with a pinch of salt.'

The family were still getting support from the public in Derby. The legal blockage they seemed to have encountered disgusted many people, and triggered off a fresh groundswell of indignation. In at least three city factories, workers signed and sent off petitions calling on the Director of Public Prosecutions to reopen the case.

But the legal blockage was soon to be unblocked. The barrister who acted for the Siddonses, Anthony Scrivener QC, felt there were grounds for an appeal against Mr Justice Schiemann's judgement. A date was set for the appeal to be heard. But it meant another year's wait for Flo and her family.

A poignant reminder of what their battle was all about came on Sunday 24 June that year as they were waiting for the appeal hearing, set down for 26 November.

Gail's daughter, Karen, had her sixteenth birthday on 24 June. Karen could barely remember her sister – she was just four when Lynn died. Now she had reached the age Lynn was at when she was killed.

Karen bought a huge bunch of flowers and the family all went out to Melbourne Cemetery to put them in Lynn's memorial vase.

Flo recalls, 'It rekindled our memories. It was a lovely thought by Karen. When they do things like that, it shows they do not forget. We will never forget.'

There was no forgetting by the people of Derby, either. Almost every time she went into the city to do her shopping, someone would stop Flo and wish her luck. Her face and those of Gail and Cynthia had appeared in the newspapers and on TV so many times they were recognised wherever they went.

Flo was walking along Harrington Street one morning after visiting her doctor, when a man shouted to her from a building site. She says, 'He used to live in Sinfin, and knew me, even though I didn't know him. He said he hoped all the fighting was not getting me down. I told him it gave me something to keep me going.'

The man then said he had once employed Mick Brookes as a labourer, but had sacked him. He said, 'He was rotten. Somebody should have poisoned him out of the way long ago.'

During the long wait Flo had difficulties getting to sleep at night. Lynn's murder was on her mind continually. When she did get to sleep, she often found herself dreaming of happier times when Lynn was alive – walking with her dog, playing records with her friends, always laughing, always bubbling with ideas, never bored or moody.

Flo's part time job as a cleaner in a solicitor's office helped to pass the time. The pay was not much. It helped towards the fares, postage and phone bills. But the real reason she kept working was to keep herself busy so that she wouldn't spend her time dwelling on Lynn's death, and feeling sorry for herself.

She also took to writing down her thoughts to pass the evenings after getting home from her job. Her sadness comes through in these writings, and so does her anger at the lawyers – although it was their job – who defended Mick and Roy Brookes. She wrote:

> Solicitors try to get such men off and make out they are hard done to. That makes me all the more determined to let Mick Brookes suffer. He did not have any pity for all he did to Lynn.
>
> Some people who have loved ones murdered say they forgive the one who did it. But me, I could never forgive or forget. I believe in an eye for an eye and so it should be.

When November came, it was time to start travelling again. She and Gail had to make several trips to London to meet lawyers preparing the case, and for the actual hearing which lasted three days in the Court of Appeal.

As usual, they got up at 5 a.m. to catch the early train from Derby. It was cheaper that way – they could save as much as £25 on their joint return fares.

On the final day – 26 November – there was a bad omen. They caught the early train from Derby and got a taxi to take them from the station to the High Court. When Gail went to pay the fare, she found she had lost her purse. She had left it at the station buffet, so there was not much chance of getting it back, and it contained both of their return tickets.

The appeal had been heard by three judges, headed by the Master of the Rolls, Lord Donaldson. He and the other two – Lord Justice Nourse and Lord Justice Russell – issued their findings in a bulky document of nearly forty pages.

But Flo and Gail didn't have to plough through it. Lord Donaldson, sitting seven feet above the two tiny women in the oak-panelled court, delivered the ruling in just five words – 'The appeal will be allowed.'

They gasped with delight. These were the words they had been waiting for, and praying they would hear. It meant their action for damages against Michael and Roy Brookes could go ahead, in spite of the earlier ruling that seemed to bring it to a peremptory stop.

There were celebrations that day in London. Solicitors, barristers, journalists and members of the Siddons family held an impromptu party across the road from the High Court at The George. Flo rarely drinks, but when Paul Foot bought a bottle of champagne, she accepted a glass.

They had time to mull over the full judgement, which decreed unanimously that the appeal should be allowed to go ahead, and that the time barrier should be lifted.

And Lord Justice Russell, in his written judgement, made a comment that gave the Siddons family and their lawyers more scope for optimism about the eventual outcome of the case.

He wrote, 'There can be no doubt that everyone concerned in the case must have understood that one or other or both of the defendants had been responsible for the attack on the girl that caused her death. No other person can conceivably be involved.'

These words had only one meaning – that a judge at the Court of Appeal had studied the evidence, and found that Mick Brookes, or Roy Brookes, or both of them together, had killed Lynn.

Gail was overjoyed. Outside the court she told a reporter, 'We've worked hard since Lynn was killed. Everytime we got somewhere we got knocked back again. This is the furthest that we've come, and we've won it. You can imagine how we're feeling at the moment.... Brilliant!'

Flo was more guarded. She said, 'I'm happy that we've got this far. I thought we might do, but I didn't say anything because it doesn't do to brag about it, does it? I'm not wild about it, but I'm glad.'

The jubilation of the family quickly spread to Derby where their friends and supporters cheered the happy news. In his weekly column in the *Evening Telegraph*, Phillip Whitehead wrote:

It is a pleasure to turn to a famous local case. The ghost of Lynn Siddons has haunted Derby and should have haunted Derbyshire police since 1978.

I first met her grandmother Florence, her mother, Gail and her Aunt Cynthia at the time of the original trial. These three women have battered at every door to find justice. I had one Attorney General tell me to my face that he believed there had been a gross miscarriage of justice.

The Siddons family moved mountains in their efforts to get the matter before a court. They had no money, no powerful lobby behind them. Yet, in the end, after many rebuffs, the Appeal Court at last listened. They will be able to bring their civil case for battery against those they believe responsible.

When I heard the verdict on Monday, I wept with joy for them. It was the same emotion the day the Berlin Wall came down. An impossible dream come true. They have made legal history. English common law will not forget them, nor will I. One day soon Lynn Siddons will sleep in peace.

As was to be expected, Michael and Roy Brookes were loath to accept the decision of the Court of Appeal. They sought leave to take the case to the House of Lords to have the judgement overturned. But leave was refused. They would have to face the accusations of the Siddons family, and try to disprove them.

Flo and Gail were in a happy mood as they went to catch their train from London that evening of 26 November twelve-and-a-half years after Lynn's death.

And their departure for Derby was made even happier. Gail inquired at St Pancras Station for her lost purse. Yes, it had been found in the cafeteria and handed in, complete with money and return tickets. Nice to know there were still some honest people about.

22   Drama in the High Court

Courtroom 22 is in the basement of the Royal Courts of Justice in the bustling heart of London. This was the court allocated for the case of Halford v. Michael and Fitzroy Brookes. The oak-panelled room, not very large, is quiet and usually cool. But it became stifling during the heatwave in July 1991, and for two days of the nine-day hearing, Mr Justice Rougier relaxed the rules and allowed the barristers to remove their wigs.

As in nearly all court hearings, however serious the underlying dispute may be, there were moments of light heartedness which produced ripples of mirth. Few of the spectators were aware that the case was making legal history. It was the first civil case in which damages were being claimed for a murder for which no one had been convicted.

The action was for battery. But the judge set the seal on the proceedings by saying, 'There's no point in mincing words. The effect of this action is to accuse the defendants of murder.'

The Siddons family were well represented. In the front row, next to their solicitor Jane Deighton, sat Flo and Gail, with the judge towering seven feet above them. Keith and Cynthia were sitting in the public gallery with their families.

The early stages were given over to lengthy arguments about what evidence was admissible, and what wasn't, and one of the first dilemmas faced by the judge was an application to order Derbyshire police to release statements and other documents relating to the case.

The police had argued that as the file on Lynn's murder was still open, releasing exhibits, original statements and statements taken long after her death could prejudice any future prosecution. The judge overruled this argument and ordered that the documents should be handed over.

The real drama came on the third day when Roy Brookes stood in the witness box and told the story, which he had told so many times before, of how he lured Lynn to her death and, even though he didn't want to, he pricked her with a knife and then watched while his stepfather strangled her and stabbed her to death.

Roy Brookes, though he was a co-defendant, had been called as a witness for the Siddonses. Their barrister, Anthony Scrivener QC, had applied for a subpoena requiring him to attend the court. This application was opposed by the barrister acting for Michael Brookes, Mr Bernard Livesey QC.

When the judge ruled Roy must attend, Mr Livesey instantly lodged an appeal. Three Appeal Court judges heard the appeal the same afternoon. They dismissed it, so Roy had to come to court.

In the witness box, he looked and sounded impressive. The court had been told of the puny wimp with a mental age of twelve who had assisted his stepfather in the murder. Now aged twenty-eight and married, he was smartly turned out in a white shirt and blue tie and he gave his evidence clearly, laconically and without hesitating.

It was galling for Flo and Gail to have to hear the horrific account of Lynn's death repeated all over again. But they were inured to it. This was not the case for some of Lynn's cousins sitting at the back. Hearing the gruesome details for the first time was too painful, and two of them left the court in tears.

Altogether, Roy Brookes gave five accounts of his part in Lynn's murder. At first, after Lynn had gone missing and before her body was found, he said that she had vanished when he went into a wood to urinate.

After Lynn was found, and he had been arrested, he had ten minutes alone with his stepfather – and then he told the story, which the police at the time believed, that he alone had stabbed Lynn after she provoked and taunted him.

The next version was the one he gave at Leicester Prison while awaiting trial. He admitted he had lured Lynn to the canal but said his stepfather had killed her, and he had played only a minimal part in the attack, gently pricking her with a knife.

Most people believed that this was the true account of what happened that fateful afternoon. It tallied with the pattern of wounds on her body and other forensic evidence. And this was the story Roy Brookes told at Nottingham Crown Court when he was tried for Lynn's murder.

After his acquittal, he was sent for a short period under a Place of Safety Order to secure accommodation at the Pastures psychiatric hospital in Mickleover, Derby. He changed his story yet again when a social worker took him to Cotton Lane police station to meet Derbyshire CID chief Det. Supt Jim Reddington.

On this occasion he reverted to version number two – that he alone had murdered Lynn and that the account he had given in court implicating his stepfather was a pack of lies.

But by the time of the High Court hearing, Roy Brookes had changed his story yet again, insisting that the true version was the one he had told at his Nottingham trial – in which the murder had been executed by Michael Brookes, and his own role had been minimal.

Just why did he change the story at the Pastures, putting forward the version that he alone was responsible for Lynn's death? Curiously, his solicitor was not present when the police began to interview him. Mr Chittenden had been told about the interview only at the last moment and was late getting there. When he did arrive, he advised Roy not to answer any more questions.

After more than six months away from his mother and sister, Roy Brookes said, 'I wanted to go home very badly. He [Mr Reddington] just wanted me to say the statement in court was not true – that if I said my first statement was true and I was going to take all the blame, it would be all over and done with – I could go home straight away and nothing more would be heard.'

The psychiatrist who interviewed Roy Brookes, Dr Tom Dorman, who at that time was based at the Pastures, was also called to give evidence. He said he was convinced that Det. Supt Reddington, under mounting public pressure to solve the crime, wanted Roy to claim he killed Lynn singlehanded.

The judge asked Dr Dorman if he thought it was a bid by the police to get a pressure group off their backs. He said, 'I was aware the police were under considerable pressure. It was my feeling that the police wanted the original statement reinstated – that Roy Brookes had carried out the killing alone – so they could get the case closed.'

A social worker present at the interview, Keith Sherwood, who was looking after Roy at the time, said the boy had been persuaded by Det. Supt Reddington's 'authoritative manner' not to implicate Michael Brookes in the belief that he might be released from the Pastures.

The judge said to Mr Sherwood, 'You have had unease from that day to this about the context in which the statement was made?' Mr Sherwood agreed.

Mr Reddington, who has now retired, was called as a witness. He told the court he had a 'perfectly clear conscience' about his conduct of the case, and he denied that he induced Roy Brookes to retract the statement in which he blamed his stepfather.

He denied he told Roy that if he reverted to the first statement in which he admitted sole responsibility, he could go home more easily.

Mr Reddington said, 'All I wanted was the truth,' adding he was sure the investigation had been conducted as well as it could have been.

He was asked about two other aspects of the police investigation into Lynn's death. Mr Scrivener asked him if the garden at the Brookes house in Carlyle Street had been dug up at the time. Mr Reddington replied that he thought it hadn't. He was also asked if forensic scientists had had a chance to examine Lynn's body before it was moved. Mr Reddington answered no.

As well as telling the High Court about his part in the murder, Roy Brookes told how his stepfather used to stalk women, threatening to 'get them' by which he meant stab them with a knife. He had said he wanted to kill more women than Jack the Ripper.

He also told how Michael Brookes used to stab pictures of women, and how he thrust his knife into a blue and yellow stuffed toy dolphin which was produced in court still showing the slashes.

Flo and Gail sat facing the front of the court and not looking at Roy in the witness box as he told of Lynn's last moments. But several times their lips quivered with emotion as the details of her death unfolded.

Roy Brookes said of his part in the knifing, 'I think I stuck it in about six times. It was like I wasn't there, like I was looking at myself doing it. It was an ever so scary feeling.'

Then, he said, as his stepfather continued the attack:

I sat down shaking and feeling sick as he knelt by her body and stuck the knife into her hard lots of times. I remember him shouting at me that she wouldn't die. I remember my dad trying to push soil into her mouth with one hand and the other hand was at the back of her neck. I remember him jumping on her head with his foot.

Roy Brookes was questioned by the judge who asked him, 'You must have realised that by taking Lynn on this walk you were leading her, if not to her death, to some horrifying experience?'

Roy answered, 'Yes.'

The judge then asked whether he did anything to warn her.

Roy answered, 'I didn't think anything was going to happen.'

The judge questioned him further, 'And is it right you stabbed her without any protest?'

'Yes,' Brookes replied.

When Roy Brookes had given his evidence, he was allowed to leave the court. Though his solicitor tried to smuggle him out through a back door holding a briefcase up to his face, he was spotted, and pursued by reporters, photographers and TV crews to the railway station where he caught a train home to Peterborough. In court the following morning, his lawyers complained. Mr Justice Rougier admonished the media for harassing him.

Earlier, the Siddons family had to go through another ordeal – hearing Professor Alan Usher, the Sheffield-based Home Office pathologist, now retired, describe Lynn's injuries.

He handed in colour-coded sketches showing the position of the stab wounds, lacerations and bruises on Lynn's body.

Dr Usher said that he found that what Roy Brookes had said in his second statement – the one implicating his stepfather – to be consistent with the injuries.

There were no defensive injuries, such as cuts on the hands or fingers as one would expect from warding off knife blows. This, said Mr Scrivener, fitted in with Roy Brookes' second statement. If there had been just one assailant, Lynn would have had at least one hand free to grasp the knife and possibly sustain defensive injuries.

Two further witnesses gave evidence about Michael Brookes and his fondness for knives. Keith Hibbert said that he knew Brookes when he was eight or nine years old, and even then he had a habit of pinning pictures of naked women on a dartboard, and throwing darts or knives at them.

Roland Cooper, a former battery sergeant major in the Royal Artillery, recalled details of visits Brookes made to his home twenty-five years previously when, as an 18-year-old, he was friendly with Mr Cooper's 15-year-old daughter, Edwina. Mr Cooper's memory couldn't be faulted. He remembered exactly how long he'd been in the army – 'twenty-two years, three months and two days'.

Brookes, he said, used to sit on the settee in his house, open magazines or catalogues, take out a knife and stab and slash pictures of scantily dressed women.

Mr Cooper said, 'I spoke to him about it. He completely and totally ignored me as if he was in a world of his own. I wanted to put the man out of the door. But my wife remonstrated. She said if I did that Edwina would meet him outside the home, and it would make them closer.'

In his closing speech, Mr Scrivener described Michael Brookes as a 'knife freak' who killed Lynn for no other reason than 'perverted sexual enjoyment'. That, he said, was the motive for Michael Brookes, and Roy Brookes was under his influence. Both of them had the opportunity, and there was the eyewitness account of the murder by Roy Brookes, and pathological evidence that more than one person had been involved.

Mr Scrivener asked, 'Apart from having a video to watch it happen, what more could you want?'

Mr Livesey, who was acting for Michael Brookes, did not call him to give evidence on his own behalf. No reason was given for this, although Mr Scrivener did say that in a civil action there was no right to silence, unlike a criminal trial.

He submitted Roy Brookes had alone committed the murder when his sexual frustration boiled over into a higher excited state. He said Roy had a drive to see in the flesh what he had seen in pictures and stabbed Lynn in a frenzy because he became hyper-excited.

Mr Justice Rougier did not give his judgement at the end of the hearing. He announced it would be reserved until the start of the new legal term in almost two months' time. But having waited almost thirteen years, Flo Siddons didn't mind waiting another few weeks.

Only once during the nine days did Flo Siddons leave the court while the hearing was in progress – and that was when Mr Livesey was defending Michael Brookes claiming that he had been wrongly accused and the evidence was such that no jury would convict him in a criminal court.

Flo admits she cannot stand to hear anyone sticking up for the Brookes – and that goes for lawyers who are engaged to defend them. So she chose this moment to go out for a cup of tea.

At the start of the hearing, Mr Scrivener said they were seeking heavy damages which could run into five figures, but Mr Livesey told the judge that the Brookes family had no money and would not be able to pay.

But Gail summed up the feeling of the whole family when she said, 'None of this is about money. I don't want his flaming money. It's about justice.'

23   No Hiding Place

TV cameramen, reporters with notebooks and tape recorders, photographers, sound engineers with their boom microphones were bunched by the railings in front of the Royal Courts of Justice on 30 September 1991. Inside Court 22 it was standing room only.

Everybody was waiting for the three stars to appear for the final scene of a drama that had gone on for thirteen years – the fight by Lynn Siddons' family to bring her cruel killers to book.

The three tiny avengers had travelled down from Derby the day before. They wanted a good night's rest before the big moment. They were not going to risk train delays or derailments making them late.

They had their lunch – sandwiches and coffee – in the Lincoln's Inn chambers of their barrister, Anthony Scrivener. Mr Scrivener, chairman of the Bar Council, much admired the pluck of the Siddons family. Every day throughout the hearings, he laid on sandwiches for them so they could have a quiet hour away from the bustle of London's pubs and cafes.

Shortly before 2 p.m. they appeared – Flo Siddons in a pale grey anorak, Gail in a smart grey and green suit and Cynthia in a bright red coat. Their clothes seemed to mirror their personalities. Fighting Flo in her anorak ready for the fray. Gail, quieter, but with a steely determination. Impetuous Cynthia in red for danger.

The reporters milled around them, and the cameras clicked away merrily as they passed through the gates to go up the steps and through the huge forbidding portals. One of the newsmen called, 'How do you think it's going to go, Flo?'

Perky as ever, the sprightly 77-year-old gave her gritty reply, 'I don't know, do I? You know as much as I do. I don't like making forecasts. We shall have to see what happens, won't we?' Inside the courtroom, an usher filled the water jug on the judge's bench. It was to take Mr Justice Rougier an hour and twenty minutes to read his findings on the case. He gave them, as he said, in great detail with a welter of reasoning in case Michael Brookes and his stepson Roy decided to appeal.

Lawyers and reporters craned forward to catch his words, as did Keith and Barrie, Cynthia and her daughters, who were sitting at the rear of the court. Gail and Flo were, as usual, at the front, sitting alongside their solicitor, Jane Deighton.

Everyone was on tenterhooks, wondering which way the judgement would go. But after reading the first few paragraphs, the judge said, 'I won't keep you in suspense any longer. I find for the plaintiffs.'

There were gasps of relief. Flo Siddons permitted herself a thin smile of triumph as she turned to face Gail. The reporter from the *Derby Evening Telegraph* stood up and pushed his way along the press bench to rush to a telephone to make sure his paper had the news the city had been waiting for in that afternoon's late edition.

The judge smiled, propped his hand under his chin, waited for the shuffling to cease, and proceeded to read his lengthy judgement. He commented on the testimony of each witness, saying why he chose to believe most of their statements. Some may have been exaggerated; others blurred by fading memories. But in essence, he said, they were true.

The judge said that while the evidence of witnesses taken in isolation was not conclusive, taken together the effect was massive.

There were only two possible scenarios for Lynn's death. One was that Roy alone killed her after she had teased him sexually, as he had claimed in his first confession. The second was that her brutal death occurred as described in his second statement – with Michael Brookes playing the dominant role and pressuring Roy to help him.

The judge listed the reasons why he thought the second was the truth of how Lynn died:

It was highly unlikely that a 16-year-old girl, especially as she was menstruating at the time, would make a pass at a boy who looked four years her junior.

The absence of defensive injuries. If Roy Brookes had been on his own, he couldn't possibly have stabbed and strangled her and prevented her hands from grabbing at the knife.

The testimony of two other witnesses, even though one, Keith Hibbert, was an old lag, that Michael Brookes had admitted to them he was the killer.

Michael Brookes' habits of stalking women and stabbing nude pictures.

The judge said that at the time of the murder Brookes was a man in the grip of demonic frenzy, and he added that Roy played his part in the killing while under duress.

But he added, 'The second defendant [Roy] did more than just prick her. The reality is he cannot admit to himself, let alone to me, what he did.'

The judge said, 'I am left in no reasonable doubt that the first defendant killed Lynn Siddons. This is a dreadful judgement to make but it is, I fear, the consequence of a dreadful crime.'

Those words were chosen by Mr Justice Rougier with great care. In a civil case, as this was, the level of proof required is the balance of probability.

A criminal case demands a higher level of proof – beyond all reasonable doubt. But the judge had decided to apply the higher standard to the evidence, the criteria for a criminal court.

He referred to the failure of Michael Brookes to testify, saying there was no right to silence in a civil action. He regarded Brookes' failure to give evidence not as being conclusive, but as having a degree of probative value.

The judge had some words to say about the police handling of the case, especially in the early stages. 'The police handling of the affair has not been entirely beyond criticism,' he said.

The damages were not assessed at the time of the judgement, but Mr Justice Rougier said that Michael Brookes was 100 per cent liable for the damages to which Lynn's estate was entitled as a result of the killing.

He also ruled that Roy was 20 per cent liable and Michael

Brookes 80 per cent liable for the pain and terror inflicted on Lynn before she died.

The judge said, 'We are told this is the first case of its type to come before the courts. Let us hope it is the last.'

After he had finished, Mr Justice Rougier thanked all those who had helped him, and then left the court. For a few seconds there was silence. Then everybody started rushing to the front to congratulate Flo and Gail.

One of the first was Phillip Whitehead, the former MP for Derby North. He had followed the case from the very beginning, and given a lot of help and support to the Siddons family. He was close to tears as he hugged and kissed Flo.

Down the years the High Court has been the scene of many dramas. Monumental defeats have been mourned in its sombre enclaves, and great victories have been celebrated. But rarely can there have been such a spectacle as the triumphant parade of the history-making Siddons family that afternoon.

Up the stairs from the basement courtroom, out through a rear door they walked, preceded by a pushing, shoving mob of photographers and TV cameramen. They were all walking backwards, of course, desperate to record every word, every facial expression, of Flo, Gail and Cynthia – and Keith and Barrie following behind.

The phalanx tumbled into Carey Street, causing traffic to brake and a motorcycle to veer. Then into Lincoln's Inn to the chambers of Anthony Scrivener where a press conference had been arranged. Reporters and photographers waited in a large room with chandeliers hanging from the ceiling. They stood on chairs and tables to get the best position.

When Flo and the rest of the family walked in, there was a spontaneous burst of applause. The Siddons' long fight seemed to touch a heartstring in the hard-bitten news gatherers. They had seen it all before. But this was different, and they clapped their hands in a rare gesture of approval.

The questions came thick and fast from all directions. Gail was asked if she was happy with the outcome. She replied, 'Yes, we are happy with the verdict. But we would not have had to do all of this in the first place if the police had done their job properly.'

Flo, in her usual gritty style, was even more critical of the police. She said, 'They made a right cock-up of it. We've taken the case this far. Now let the police get on with it.'

Cynthia told the BBC reporter, 'I still can't believe we've won. My legs are shaking. We've been knocked back many times but now we've done it. Most of it's down to my mum's determination – she's a great woman.'

Jane Deighton's background performance throughout the long campaign has won praise from legal experts. Most of the time she was content to stay in the background. But on this occasion she took her brightly illuminated place in the TV lights next to the family she steered to victory.

Jane had her own comment to make:

> It must be asked why these two women managed to piece together the evidence they needed to build the case against Michael Brookes, and why it was the police took no notice of that evidence. Why was it the Director of Public Prosecutions refused to prosecute even when these two women had dug their evidence up, pieced it together and built a case? These questions must be answered.

It was left to Flo to sum up the feelings of the family – and what action they felt should now be taken against Michael Brookes after he had been named by the judge as Lynn's killer.

Flo thought for a moment. Then she said, 'Well, we're very happy with what the judge said. I think he got it right. As for Michael Brookes, there should now be a criminal prosecution against him. I could never forgive anybody who did what he did to Lynn, or anybody else. He should go to prison. For a long time. A very long time.'

Eighty-two miles away, a less formal press conference was taking place on a housing estate on the outskirts of Peterborough. The newspapers had tracked down Michael Brookes, even though he had sought anonymity under the assumed name of Michael Goodwood.

At first the reporters were not made at all welcome. Mick's shrieking wife, Dot, chased the man from the *Derby Evening Telegraph* out of the garden, hurling a bucket of water over him and screaming, 'Piss off. Leave us alone'.

But the reporters came back. And Brookes gave a few grudging comments while hiding behind the frosted glass of a bathroom window hoping his face would not be recognized.

One of the reporters shouted, 'Will you tell us in your own words you didn't kill Lynn Siddons?'

From the slightly open window Dot Brookes bawled, 'We've already told you that.'

Brookes accused the Siddons family of plotting to murder him. Again from the bathroom window he shouted, 'Ask them what about the threat to murder me and my daughter. Go on, ask 'em.'

When she was told about this, Flo Siddons said, 'It's a load of rubbish. He's a liar, isn't he? It was a premeditated murder. If he's innocent, he should stand up and prove his innocence.'

Brookes was determined to keep his face hidden. After being labelled a murderer by a High Court judge, he didn't want people in his neighbourhood where he had worked as a window cleaner recognizing him.

He gave a short interview to Central Television with his face blacked out. In the interview he said, 'The witnesses who have been in that court have done nothing but tell lies. I just don't know what to do. I am unemployed. I have no money. I have got nothing.

'The last thirteen years have been hell. Certain men have tried to kill me. Every time I go out I look over my shoulder.'

But Brookes didn't know a camera team from BBC television had positioned themselves in a neighbour's bedroom for two days with zoom lenses trained on his front door. When he stepped outside to tinker with his car, they got the shots they had been patiently waiting for.

The face was slightly fatter than in previous pictures taken eleven years earlier shortly after Lynn's death. Then he looked gaunt, with lank dark curls hanging over his forehead. Now the hair was greying, with a bald patch.

Those pictures appeared on television, and on the front pages of nearly every newspaper the next morning. Michael Brookes' attempts to conceal his identity had been in vain.

There was no hiding place for him. He would have to face his accusers – and the world.

24   A Promise Kept

Almost a year before her High Court victory, Flo Siddons
sat at the table in her front room one evening with a pen and
pad, and gazed wistfully at her favourite picture of Lynn.
She kept it in the middle of the mantelpiece – it shows the
teenager with her mischievous, slightly crooked grin in a
green bikini swimming costume. It was taken on the family's
last holiday together at Tenby. Flo sighed and looked away
from the picture. Then she began to write a letter in her
neat, clear hand.

Flo was used to letter writing. She wrote hundreds of
letters during the thirteen-year campaign following her
granddaughter's death. Mostly she wrote late in the evening.
That was the best time when things were quiet – and she
couldn't get to sleep anyway with Lynn's murder constantly
on her mind.

Over the years, she had written to the five chief constables
of Derbyshire who had held the job since Lynn's death in
1978. Now a new chief constable had been appointed. Flo
wanted to make sure he knew all about Lynn, and the
family's dissatisfaction with the way the police had handled
the murder investigation.

Slowly the pen moved over the blue notepaper:

Dear Mr Newing,
    I do not know how much you know of the murder of my
granddaughter Lynn Siddons who was murdered April 3rd,
1978, and my family and myself have been fighting to get the
killer to justice. Over the years Derbyshire police have not
been interested in following up the case. With you being
made the new Chief Constable and coming from London,
you might be more interested to help us.

172

The next morning on her way into Derby, Flo posted the letter to the police headquarters at Ripley. She expected the usual reply – a stock letter saying the police were doing all they could – but she was in for a surprise.

A message arrived that the Chief Constable would like to see her – when would be a convenient time for him to call? Within a couple of days a police car came swishing through the snow. It pulled up outside her house and there almost filling the doorway was the large frame of John Newing.

Flo greeted him, 'Come on in. I'm pleased to meet you.'

Newing looked down at the diminutive letter writer. He smiled, 'Nice to meet you, too.'

Flo and the Chief Constable sat in her front room talking about the case for almost an hour. He told her that with the civil case pending, his officers could not take immediate action. But he promised her that when the High Court hearing was concluded, he would do whatever he could to close the book on the unsolved murder case.

John Newing said after the meeting:

> The investigation is open and current. As soon as we are in a position to take the matter forward, and we can't take it forward while the civil case is going on, we shall seek to follow the advice we have been given by the Director of Public Prosecutions who will then make a decision if the matter can be put before the court again.

He was told that the Siddons family felt they had had a raw deal from the police. He replied, 'I can understand why Mrs Siddons feels like that. I want to make sure we finally get the matter properly resolved. That is an objective not just that I've got, but that a lot of my officers have got. They would like to see this case closed. And there is only one way to close a murder case.'

John Newing was as good as his word. He had an officer, Det. Supt. Ron McAllister at the High Court hearing. As soon as it was over, McAllister phoned him with the result.

That very day Newing arranged for two of his senior officers to go to the offices of the Director of Public Prosecutions with the updated police file on the murder.

He said how pleased he was the Siddons family had won

their case, but he hinted the result may have hindered rather than helped the chances of a successful criminal prosecution.

'I believe it is going to be extremely difficult, in view of the Judge's remarks in court, for any person charged with this offence, especially if his name is Michael Brookes, to get a fair hearing. The Director of Public Prosecutions will have to pay regard to that.'

Newing also answered criticisms of his police force, even though he was not involved with it at the time of the murder. He said:

> To err is human. We are all capable of making mistakes. What we have to recognise is that when mistakes are made, they have to be admitted. That does not mean the people responsible for those mistakes are bad people, nor that they are unprofessional. It means they have made mistakes. When you look at their record through a lifetime of policing, it has been very good indeed.
>
> On this occasion it wasn't up to the normal professional standards you would associate with a murder investigation, or any other criminal investigation for that matter.

John Newing, like other law enforcers, felt that the major error was not charging Michael Brookes at the same time as Roy, or at least, after Roy had made his second statement implicating his stepfather. He commented, 'With the benefit of hindsight, Brookes should have been charged at the time, but he wasn't.'

The man who was in charge of the investigation, Det. Superintendent Jim Reddington, who has retired, disclosed after the High Court decision that he had wanted to charge both Michael and Roy Brookes with Lynn's murder. But his recommendation that they should be jointly charged was turned down by the Director of Public Prosecutions who said there was not enough evidence for Michael Brookes to be put on trial.

Reddington was also asked to comment on criticisms of the way he and other officers carried out the investigation. He replied:

> It was a very difficult investigation. All sorts of problems sprang up from time to time, and we dealt with them the best way we knew how at the time. I think if it happened again,

we'd probably do exactly the same thing. It's been very difficult. I feel very sorry for the victim's relatives and I can understand their feelings but we did our best.

It was a best, unfortunately, that allowed a killer to remain free, even if the wrath of the avenging Siddons family has, as Brookes says, made his life a misery.

The view has been put forward by many people that if Michael Brookes had confessed at the time, faced his trial, and been sentenced to life imprisonment, he would, by now, almost certainly have been freed, having paid the penalty for the crime. But he has persisted in protesting his innocence, as he did after the High Court judge had decreed him guilty of murder.

With his cover blown by the newspaper pictures showing him as he looks today, Brookes emerged with his solicitor the day after the judgement was announced. There was no point in continuing to hide, so he decided to face the cameras.

The talking, however, was left to his solicitor, Anthony Wharton, who read out a lengthy statement:

> Mr Justice Rougier's findings do not amount to a criminal verdict of guilty, although the widespread reports and comments in today's newspapers would have it otherwise.
>
> It's our view that there were a number of irregularities in the conduct of the plaintiff's case which are causing us to review the judgement with care with a view to taking the matter to appeal.
>
> The media should now desist and leave Michael Brookes alone. He is not going to be interviewed at this juncture. If he were, he would repeat his denials of responsibility for this dreadful murder although I appreciate that such denials would be like spitting in the wind in view of the long campaign of public vilification against him.

Mr Wharton also said that after thirteen years of incessant publicity, it would be quite impossible for Brookes to get a fair trial. 'Anyone who thinks he could get a fair trial is deluding themselves,' he added.

There were mixed views on this. Some legal experts, including the controversial Judge James Pickles, believed Michael Brookes could get a fair trial. All that would be needed, he said in a TV interview, would be for the judge to direct the jury to disregard what they had read in newspapers and make up their minds on the evidence presented.

But others took a different view. They argued that it would be virtually impossible to find a jury who had not heard of the case – and were not aware that a High Court judge had found Brookes guilty of the murder in the civil court. Even with direction, it would be a very unusual juror who could cast it out of his or her mind, and remain unprejudiced.

It took the legal experts a couple of months to work out exactly what compensation should be paid to the Siddons family for Lynn's death, and the years of anguish that followed it.

There are strict guidelines laid down in law for calculating such a claim. It is based on the victim's earning potential, and how much Lynn might have contributed towards family finances were it not for her early demise.

But when they heard the amount – £10,641 – Flo and Gail were shocked. As they had said many times, they weren't in the game for the money. The motive that sustained them was to get justice. But nevertheless the paltriness of the award angered them.

The announcement came soon after a libel jury awarded £60,000 to William Roache, the actor who plays Ken Barlow in *Coronation Street*, after a newspaper had called him, among other things, boring.

After the Siddons award, Gail fumed, 'It's disgusting. You can get £60,000 for being called boring. Yet Lynn is murdered, and all the law allows us is under £11,000. It's a stupid law. It should be changed.'

Many people have paid tribute to the spirit of the Siddons family for their tenacity and persistence in the campaign to get justice for Lynn. The gutsy trio of Flo, Gail and Cynthia have won praise from lawyers, police officers, journalists, politicians and, above all, from the ordinary people of Derby – the people whose sympathy, support and friendship they have won by their determination.

One of the most eloquent tributes came from Phillip Whitehead who said:

I think Flo Siddons is one of the most remarkable women I've known. I met her first under the shadow of enormous tragedy. She had brought Lynn up, and her murder and the horrific circumstances would have shaken any family. They devastated Mrs Siddons, and her daughters Gail and Cynthia and the rest of the family. I know they were all deeply shaken by it.

But to see this woman over the next twelve years enter her old age fighting for a cause, educating herself in the ways of the law, buttonholing journalists, appealing to MPs, going endlessly down to London, and simply doggedly saying one thing: *The murderer of Lynn Siddons is still walking the streets a free man. The law should not allow this. He has to be brought to justice.*

And eventually people listen.

Somebody, it seemed, did listen. There was a new Director of Public Prosecutions sitting in the office in Queen Anne's Gate in London. For the first time, a woman had been appointed to the post, Mrs Barbara Mills QC. Shortly after she took over, the file on Lynn Siddons landed on her desk.

Before giving the go-ahead for a criminal case to proceed, the Director of Public Prosecutions needs to feel sure it has a 51 per cent chance of succeeding. The question was, would a woman take a different view from her predecessors who had five times ruled the case was not strong enough for a criminal prosecution of Michael Brookes?

25 'You're Nicked!'

Phil Hartley was busy as was every other detective in Derby in the first week of July, 1992. An Asian had been stabbed in a street brawl, and a lot of enquiries had to be made. But the order that crackled over his car radio in the afternoon of 7 July overrode all other tasks. It was his boss, Det. Supt. Ron McAllister, 'Get down to The Bunker. Quickly!'

Beneath Derby's Cotton Street Police Station is a spacious room where large numbers of officers assemble for murder cases or other serious crimes. A smaller room leads off it, where the officer in control can keep an eye on his team. This room is nicknamed The Bunker.

When Det. Sgt. Hartley arrived, he found McAllister and the head of Derbyshire CID, Det. Chief Supt. Duncan Bailey waiting. They had received a telephone call from the headquarters of the Crown Prosecution Service, and they said to Hartley, 'We want you to arrest Michael Brookes, bring him back to Derby and charge him with the murder of Lynn Siddons.'

Fourteen years and three months had elapsed since Lynn's death. At the time, Hartley was a young policeman on traffic patrol. But he had become more involved in the case when he moved to CID, and took charge of the file of statements in readiness for the civil action Lynn's family took against Brookes.

Publicity following the judgment by Mr Justice Rougier had brought another witness forward – David Groves, who had provided Roy Brookes with lodgings at his Peterborough home. Groves claimed Roy had told him about the murder, and how his stepfather went berserk and kept stabbing Lynn.

Groves then said he had gone round to Michael Brookes'

house and confronted him. Brookes denied he had done the murder but, according to Groves, said that Roy had started the stabbing and he carried on to make sure Lynn was dead so that she could not identify her killers.

Groves had gone to the local police with his story, but had been ignored. In the welter of publicity following the civil action, he contacted the police again. This time a detective from Derby travelled to Peterborough to see him.

As Groves told his story, the detective realized it could be vital. Even though Brookes had claimed Roy was the killer, his own words were now placing him at the scene of the crime – something he had always vehemently denied.

Phil Hartley knew all about the ramifications of the case. He took three detectives with him and arranged for two other cars of drug squad officers to follow. They were briefed to carry out a minute search of Brookes' house. Hartley had chosen well – no detectives are better at searching than those used to looking for minute packets of hidden drugs.

The convoy set off for the one-and-a-half-hour drive from Derby to Peterborough. They had arranged a rendezvous in a hotel car-park with local police officers who piloted them to the house in Goldhay where Michael Brookes had lived under the name of Goodwood since he left Derby.

Hartley looked at his watch as he knocked at 128 Howland. It was ten past eight. The door was opened by Dot Brookes' mother. Hartley told her who he was, and she let him and another detective, Ian Penman, into the house. They walked through to the living-room where Mick Brookes and Dot were sitting on the settee watching TV.

Hartley knew how, at the various court hearings, the country's top lawyers had clashed over the case. He had been briefed to play the arrest strictly by the book. The last thing the police wanted was a barrister arguing about some legal technicality in the arrest procedure. The words came from his mouth as if a record was playing:

'Michael Brookes, I am Detective Sergeant Hartley from Derby CID. I am arresting you for the murder of Lynn Siddons. (Pause) You don't have to say anything but I must warn you that anything you do say may be given in evidence.'

Brookes didn't utter a sound, but the colour drained from his face and he looked stunned. His wife, however, made up for his silence. She began to rant, 'He didn't do it, you bastards. Fuck off out of here. Leave us alone.'

While Brookes went upstairs to change his clothes, Dot rang his solicitor. She was still talking when Brookes came down. He was taken between two detectives to the waiting police car.

The journey back to Derby took place in almost total silence. Hartley had instructed his men not to exchange a single word with their prisoner. Once or twice Brookes tried to start a conversation but there was no response from the stony-faced officers.

Brookes was processed at Full Street Police Station, searched and placed in a cell. Shortly afterwards the cars arrived with the search team. They had found a plastic bag full of press cuttings referring to the Lynn Siddons case, and also a paperback about the Yorkshire Ripper.

Sgt. Hartley was not displeased with the evening's work. The bag of cuttings helped to substantiate the story David Groves had told of seeing a scrapbook full of newspaper stories about the case. Brookes was allowed his mandatory phone call – he rang Dot. Finally he was photographed, fingerprinted and taken back to his cell.

Flo Siddons was delighted when she heard of Brookes' arrest. But her years of campaigning, when so often her rising hopes had been cruelly dashed, had taught her to be guarded in her optimism.

When Michael Brookes appeared briefly before Derby magistrates the following morning and was driven off to Leicester Prison with a blanket over his head, it looked as if the Lynn Siddons case might be drawing towards its conclusion. But there were to be four more years of legal wrangling before he would be put on trial.

During this time the name of Michael Brookes vanished from the headlines. The High Court imposed a ban on the legal arguments being reported, because the judges felt any further publicity could prejudice the trial.

The first move by Brookes' lawyers was to apply for a stay of the legal process against him. The case was deemed too complex for lay magistrates, and a stipendiary magistrate,

Michael James, was brought into Derby from Birmingham to hear the application.

They put forward two arguments for a stay. The first was the length of time since the murder; the memories of witnesses would have faded making their testimonies unreliable.

The second argument was the vast amount of publicity that had been given to the case. The lawyers reeled out masses of published material which they said would be bound to colour the minds of potential jurors.

The stipendiary magistrate listened patiently to these arguments, but ruled against them. 'Memories may cloud with the passage of time,' he said, 'but not with events as dramatic as murder.' They would remain in vivid relief like looking down the wrong end of a telescope where the object seems further away but is much more sharply defined.

He also overruled the publicity argument. 'Newspaper headlines are quickly forgotten by most of the public,' he said, 'and jurors can be directed by the trial judge to put out of their minds anything they may have read about the case.'

Michael Brookes was not languishing in gaol while the lawyers argued. He applied for bail and was sent to a bail hostel in Carlisle with a condition that he should not step outside Cumbria except to attend court. Later he was allocated a council house in Carlisle so Dot could live with him but the family had to move when neighbours discovered who he was and smashed the windows.

His legal team decided to contest the decision by the stipendiary magistrate that the trial should be allowed to go ahead, and they went to the High Court in London in February 1993. But the High Court judges refused their application for a judicial review, ruling that the trial must go ahead.

Almost two years after he was arrested, on 20 June 1994, the committal proceedings began. Brookes was not there to hear them. He produced a doctor's note saying he was suffering from stress and could not attend.

The stipendiary magistrate went ahead, hearing all the witnesses to decide if there was a prima-facie case to commit Brookes for trial. But a major hitch brought along another long delay when Roy Brookes refused to allow records of conversations with his solicitors to be disclosed to the court.

Such documents are privileged, and Roy Brookes steadfastly refused to waive that privilege. The argument went first to the Appeal Court, and then to the highest court in the land – the House of Lords.

After a four-day hearing the Law Lords came down on the side of Roy Brookes. It was his right, they decreed, to decide whether the documents should be disclosed to the court. He chose not to.

The committal went ahead on 21 August 1995. Michael Brookes, the magistrate decided, must face his trial – the final step in the long campaign to get justice for Lynn.

26　A Prayer Answered

It's only a short walk from our most famous court, the Old
Bailey, to our most famous church, St Paul's Cathedral.
Even though her arthritic knee was troubling her, Flo
Siddons insisted on taking that walk on the final day of
Michael Brookes' murder trial.

It had gone on for more than six weeks, and the jury had
been out considering the case for more than six hours. Their
verdict could come at any time. Everyone was on
tenterhooks with most of the seasoned court reporters laying
odds that Brookes would be acquitted.

Flo was tired. She hadn't had a wink of sleep the previous
night. Those long hot days in Court 2, especially listening to
the interminable wrangling of the lawyers, were beginning to
wear her down.

During the lunch-break she and her family walked along
the street and up the steps and into St Paul's. They knelt
down and prayed. They prayed for justice; they prayed that
at the end of their eighteen-year wait Lynn's killer would get
his just deserts. And then they lit a candle for Lynn.

They didn't have to wait much longer. After eight hours
and fifty-one minutes, the four women and eight men on the
jury came back into the court. The foreman was asked if
they had reached a verdict. 'We have,' he said. 'Guilty.'

Brookes showed little emotion. He was led down the
thirteen steps from the dock to begin the mandatory life
sentence for the murder. Everyone crowded around Flo to
congratulate her. She allowed herself a thin smile as she
said, 'Our prayers have been answered. I shall die a happy
woman. But not just yet.'

And she revealed that for years she had been keeping a
bottle of champagne for this day. 'I'll have a little drink

when I get home,' she said. 'But not too much. To tell you the truth, I don't like the taste of the stuff.'

The trial had started on 17 June 1996 almost four years after Brookes' arrest. The Old Bailey in London was chosen as the venue. It had to be well away from Derby where most of the population would remember the murder and an unprejudiced jury would have been almost impossible to find.

Brookes had grown a shaggy beard. Before the trial started, he had heard his counsel, Jonathan Goldberg, QC, describe him as a depressed, moronic figure who would not be giving evidence on his own behalf after a psychiatrist had examined him and declared him unfit to do so.

This information was given to the judge, Mr Justice Mitchell, before the jury was sworn in. But it was contested by the prosecution. A second doctor said Brookes was capable of giving evidence. In the end his defence elected not to call him – an action from which the jury could draw their own inference.

There were three days of legal arguments and submissions before the trial proper started. At one stage it looked as if it might collapse, Roy Brookes was still maintaining his right not to disclose records of dealings with his solicitor.

Mr Goldberg questioned him ferociously about his motive for maintaining this stance asking was he not concerned the jury might think he had something to hide. But Roy Brookes continued to refuse to divulge what was in these documents.

Fearing that it might bring about a premature end to the trial, Gail Halford approached Roy during a lunch-break. 'Help us, please,' she begged. Like everyone else involved in the case, she knew Roy's testimony was vital if his stepfather was to be convicted. But he shrugged his shoulders and walked away.

Roy did admit, under cross-examination, that one of the secrets in those documents was a warning from his solicitor that his mother, whom he adored, might get into trouble and face charges herself unless he put the blame where it belonged – on Michael Brookes.

Roy was the chief witness for the prosecution, which was conducted by Anthony Palmer, QC. The story that he told describing how his stepfather had strangled and stabbed

Lynn was a repeat of his testimony at his own trial in Nottingham in 1978.

It was when he was being cross-examined by Jonathan Goldberg, a formidable interrogator, that the trial suddenly became dramatic. Goldberg's rasping questions zipped across the tense courtroom:

Q: You have got clean away with murder?

A: No.

Q: You murdered this girl alone?

A: No.

Q: In a sexual frenzy?

A: No.

Q: And because she called you a black bastard?

A: No.

Q: And you invented the story involving your father as a defence at your trial?

A: No.

Roy Brookes would not be moved. A puny wimp he may have been at the time of Lynn's murder but now, aged thirty-three, he was his own man. He stuck to his story and described the killing exactly as he had described it at his own trial eighteen years before.

As a witness, Flo was allowed to sit in court but other members of the family had to sit in the public gallery. Flo took her seat a few paces from Michael Brookes. On one occasion his close presence proved too much for her and she blurted out, 'You're pathetic!'

It brought her a rebuke from a police officer, but she didn't mend her ways. Later she had a go at Jonathan Goldberg letting him know her views on lawyers who speak up for murderers.

Court officials decided they couldn't have her venting her feelings at all and sundry. Not even the judge felt safe! So an usher was deputed to sit by her and to keep her in order. It caused the family much amusement – 'Here comes Mum and her minder,' quipped Gail.

An Old Bailey trial costs an estimated £100 a minute – £30,000 a day. The Brookes trial lasted for thirty-four days – more than £1 million. Altogether, the cost of the Siddons case with all the other court hearings and investigations has been estimated to exceed £5 million.

Much of the evidence was a repeat of earlier hearings. The pathologist, Dr Alan Usher, spoke of Lynn's injuries. He said it was possible one person could have killed her but, as she was stabbed and strangled simultaneously, two people was a more likely scenario. He also said the pattern of wounding suggested a left-handed knifeman.

The jury passed a note to the judge asking if Michael Brookes was left-handed. The answer came back, 'Yes'. Roy Brookes, it was pointed out, is right-handed.

Mr Justice Mitchell took three days to sum up the case. His directions to the jury were meticulous in their fairness. He also stressed what a difficult job they would have in assessing who was telling the truth and who was lying, and making up their minds who did kill Lynn.

It *was* a difficult job. They came back twice; once to ask the judge if he would accept a majority verdict – so at least one of them felt the case against Brookes had not been proved; the second time they still couldn't make up their minds, so the judge sent them for a walk.

A wise judge! A thirty-minute stroll around the City streets was just what they needed. They returned with their verdict. Gail Halford burst into tears when it was finally announced. So did her sister, Cynthia Smith. The sudden release after years of pressure was too much for them. But they recovered when they went outside the court where a battery of TV cameras was awaiting them.

Flo, by now eighty-one years old, spoke for them all. 'It's taken a long time but in the end justice has been done. We're very grateful to everyone who supported us.' Cynthia added, 'Especially the people of Derby.'

Even before the trial students were studying the Lynn Siddons case. It has appeared on the syllabus of law classes at night schools. There are many lessons to be learned from it – by the police and by our law makers.

Surely it has to be wrong that the only way justice can be achieved and a killer brought to book is by a long and wearisome campaign by an elderly woman and her family.

Even the police agree that Michael Brookes would still be a free man if it were not for Flo Siddons and her gritty persistence. Who knows? Having got away with it once, perhaps he might have been tempted to lure some other hapless young girl to a lonely place and slaughter her to satiate his lust.

He wrecked many lives when he took Lynn's. He wrecked his stepson's life by the cowardly way he tried to bully him to take the blame; he wrecked the happy family life of the Siddons; he wrecked the lives of his own family. But, most of all, he wrecked his own life.

He shambled from the dock a wretched figure to start his sentence. Since Lynn's death he had moved home a total of fourteen times. The campaign by her family had turned him into a reclusive nomad who spent his days watching videos, afraid to step into the street.

But now the Siddons family could put him out of their minds. They didn't give him a thought when, shortly after the end of the trial, Flo, Gail and Cynthia went to Melbourne Cemetery. A summer breeze was rustling through the branches of the tall spruce tree which overlooks the Garden of Remembrance.

They put fresh flowers in Lynn's vase. The inscription simply says: *Lynn Siddons, April 3rd, 1978.* There is no mention of how she met her death.

The three women stood in silence for a few minutes. There were no words to be said. Then they went home. Their task was complete. There was nothing more to be done.

Index

189

190 · INDEX ·

Derby Evening Telegraph, 26, 29, 136, 151, 157, 167, 170
Derby Trader, 103, 108
Derbyshire County Council, 83
Derbyshire police, 82, 134–5, 138–45
diatom identification, 144
Director of Public Prosecutions, 85, 106–7, 140, 142, 146–7, 154, 173–4, 177
Donaldson, Lord, 156
Dorman, Dr Tom, 34–5, 54, 161–2
Draycott, Douglas, QC, 53–6, 59, 66, 67
Dunworth, Carol, 89, 95, 110, 119, 140

Edmunds, Pat, 43–4

fair trial, 174
fortune teller, 44
Foot, Paul, 130–7, 141, 146, 156
funeral of Lynn Siddons, 50–1

Gilseman, Nick, 150
Goldberg, Jonathan, QC, 184–5
Goodman, Helen, 93
Goodwood, Michael (Michael Brookes' alias), 110, 112, 170, 179
Greyhound, The, 43
Groves, David, 178–9
Gunn, Sheila, 48

Hailsham, Lord, 153
Halford, Gail, 12, 20–1, 27
Lynn's birth, 38–40, 72, 77–8, 81, 82, 84, 88, 90, 95–6, 130, 148, 149, 152, 153, 156, 157, 165, 176, 184, 185, 186, 187
Halford, John, 88, 95–7
Halford, Karen, 154
Hamilton, Graham, QC, 52, 68
Hardwick, Ian, 31
Hartley, Det. Sgt. Phil, 178–180
Havers, Sir Michael, 106–7, 122
Hawcroft, Bernard, 101–2
Hibbert, Keith, 103–5, 109, 122, 132, 164, 168

High Court, 159, 166–9
Home Secretary, 128–9
Hoon, Geoffrey, 153

Jack the Ripper, 162
James, Michael, 181
Judges' Rules, 143, 147
Jimmy's bar (St James' Hotel), 104

Knight, Greg, 148

Lamb, Lady Caroline, 73
Lamb, William, 73
Lassie (Lynn's dog), 19
Law Society, 148
Legal Aid, 148
Leicester Prison, 34, 35, 103, 180
Livesey, Bernard, QC, 160, 164
Lloyd, Ossie, 90, 93
Long Eaton, 119
Lowe, Cllr Harry, 139

Mablethorpe, 89, 93, 95
McAllister, Det. Supt. Ron, 173, 178
McCrea, Paul, 136
Macklin Street, 81, 82, 87–90
Mais, Mr Justice, 52, 58, 68
Manchester High Court, 152
Master of the Rolls, 156
mediums, 125
Meehan, Andy, 150
Meehan, Carl, 150
Meir, Kath, 42–3
Melbourne, 73
cemetery, 51, 71–2, 154, 187
Melbourne, Viscount, 73
Merseyside police, 139–42
Miles, Tony, 133
Miller, Ernest, 139
Mills, Barbara, QC, 177
Mitchell, Mr Justice, 184, 186
Morley, Shane, 114–15
Morton, Det. Insp. Roy, 106, 113
Muir, Bobby, 17, 23, 25, 27

Newing, John, 172–4
Nottingham Crown Court, 52
Nourse, Lord Justice, 156